SALT

NOT MUSTARD

and other thoughts
on being church

BRUCE MANNERS

SIGNS
PUBLISHING
COMPANY

Printed and published by
SIGNS PUBLISHING COMPANY
Warburton, Victoria

Copyright © 2005 by Signs Publishing Company.

All rights reserved. Except as provided under Australian copyright law no part of this book may be reproduced in any way without permission in writing from the publishers.

Unless otherwise stated, all Bible quotations are taken from the *Holy Bible, New International Version*. Copyright © 1973, 1978, 1984 by International Bible Society. Used by permission of Hodder & Stoughton Ltd, a member of the Hodder Headline Plc Group. All rights reserved.

Bible quotations marked NLT are from the *Holy Bible, New Living Translation*, copyright © 1996. Used by permission of Tyndale House Publishers, Inc, Wheaton, Illinois 60189. All rights reserved.

Bible quotations marked KJV are from the Authorised King James Version.

This book was
Edited by Graeme H Brown
Cover design by Kathy Chee
Front cover photo by Angela Brown
Back cover photo by Hedley Anderson
Text design by Heather Jones
Typeset in 10.5/14.5 Berkeley Book

ISBN 1 876010 83 5

Dedication

Dedicated to the people at Signs Publishing Company who polish, process, print, publish and package the products created there. They are a delightful group of people.

INTRODUCTION AND
ACKNOWLEDGEMENTS

"Do you believe everything you write?" I'm not sure what was behind the question, but I rank it as one of the oddest questions I've been asked about my writing. Odd because I thought believing what you wrote, at least in my area of writing, was understood. That it was a given.

You can take that as a given in what follows. Collected from editorials appearing in *Record* over a 17-year period (1988-2004), some have been updated, but the basic content and message in them have remained.

Both my predecessor and successor as editor of *Record* need to take some responsibility for this book appearing. James Coffin invited me to work on the editorial team. Jim is not only an excellent writer and editor, but proved to be a skilled teacher in the processes of both. The four years we worked together were invaluable training for me.

Nathan Brown, my successor, made the suggestion that people might actually have an interest in reading a collection of my editorials. I thank him for the suggestion and his support of the project.

Thanks also go to Graeme Brown (not related to Nathan), book editor for Signs Publishing Company. In this role he has worked most directly on the project as it has gone through the various processes to the in-your-hand stage. His careful reading, correcting, suggesting and editing have proved invaluable.

Special thanks to Chris Winzenried, who compiled this collection while working as an intern at Signs Publishing Company.

Through my years on the editorial team we had great people on the team. It tended to be more like a group of friends who happened to work together than a "real" workplace. Their suggestions and their original editorial work on my editorials have also helped polish what appears here. Thank you.

CONTENTS

A THEOLOGY OF COMMONSENSE

Developing a theology of commonsense *1*
The challenge of "present truth" *3*
When theology goes pop *6*
Let's not get trigger happy *8*
The beast, bar codes and Bill Gates *10*
Vanishing hitchhikers and signs of hell *12*
Einstein and taking truth to the limit *14*
From fear to glory *16*
A plumber goes a-plumbing *18*
Keeping the theology simple *20*

CHURCH WAS SIMPLE ... WHEN?

Church was simple . . . when? *23*
Why bother with church? *26*
Consuming passions *28*
Living in the land of the bland *30*
Christ at Christmas? Yes, please! *33*
In praise of city living *35*
Here's to responsible drinking *37*
Should churches be accountable? *39*
Should we fear change? *42*
Dollar-driven church? *44*

SALT, NOT MUSTARD

Salt, not mustard *47*
Sin and sinners *49*
The human touch *52*
If you were a guest to your church . . . *54*
Lessons from an Olympic experience *56*
The Caroline Davis I never knew *59*
The Fred Phelps School of Evangelism *61*
Swoosh, fish, cross & U *63*
Jesus in pinstripes *65*
Next door to David Gray *68*
The outsider *70*

ORDINARY SAINTS

Ordinary saints *73*
Thoughts on *Bruce Almighty* *75*
The ultimate reality *77*
The miracle of life *80*
When you wonder about God *82*
Three funerals and a resurrection *84*
Rabbi Fred's secret of success *86*
Parable of two parents *88*
How goes the battle? *91*
How far from Eden? *93*
But . . . *95*
Peter *97*

NEVER DROPPING OUR ARMS

Never dropping our arms *99*
Where are the big-idea people? *101*
Crippled minds *104*
Just another marriage breakdown *107*
Seen, but not . . . what? *109*
Married *and* happy? *111*
Permanent outcasts? *113*
Fair go, pew sitter *115*
Fair go, preacher *117*

THE WORLD HAS CHANGED

The world has changed *121*
Elvis, Dolly and a dilemma *123*
Questions from a killing field *126*
Being Christian about suicide *128*
Lessons from Waco—1 *130*
Lessons from Waco—2 *132*
On sexual abuse *134*
Gun control—vain hope? *136*

A THEOLOGY
OF COMMONSENSE

DEVELOPING A THEOLOGY
OF COMMONSENSE

Twenty-three-year-old Spencer Evans was bitten by a rattlesnake as he led a revival meeting in North Georgia.

"It hit my wrist. It was like a baseball popped me," said Evans. "I was preachin', just comin' to the end of my message. It was dark out, and I wasn't watchin' it."

Although he wasn't keen on it, medics took him to a hospital where they had to fight to save his arm and his life.

"I done took 'em [snakes] up," he said after his release. "I still believe it's right. The Bible didn't say they wouldn't bite" (www.augustachronicle.com).

Evans was following in the tradition of George W Hensley, an illiterate Tennessee preacher who claimed to be the first, at least in modern times, to make snake-handling a part of his faith. He reasoned that Pentecostals believed in exorcisms, speaking in new tongues and laying hands on the sick; so why not in taking up serpents?

He preached on Mark 16:18 one Sunday in 1910 and concluded his sermon by taking a large rattlesnake out of a box with his bare hands. He handled it for several minutes, then ordered his congregation to handle it too or be "doomed to eternal hell" (Ted Olsen, *Christian History*).

Hensley eventually died—from snakebite—on July 25, 1955, in Florida at the age of 70. It's estimated that 2000 in the Appalachian area of the United States still incorporate handling snakes and drinking strychnine as a "salvation cocktail" into their faith and worship, with about 200 actively practising the faith tests.

Their belief is based on the words of Jesus (in Mark 16:18 and Luke 10:19) that snakes wouldn't harm and poisons wouldn't hurt them when on mission service. The interpretation given by these snake-handlers is probably the strangest illustration of theology lacking in commonsense.

When Jesus was tempted to jump from the temple peak, He responded with, "The Scriptures also say, 'Do not test the Lord your God'" (Luke 4:12, NLT). Were the 100 or so who have died from snakebite in the past 90 years lacking in faith? Or was it a natural consequence of stupidity (which, being translated, is a lack of commonsense) in that they presumed to test God?

Developing a theology of commonsense in no way belittles or changes the grand themes and teachings of the Bible. They are the certainties upon which we build our Christian life. Commonsense has its place. It can be illustrated in a minor way when you look around your church and find women without hats or scarves when they pray. The reasons for Paul's counsel that women should wear head coverings (1 Corinthians 11:4-10, NLT) are no longer valid.

The impact of commonsense with theology is seen in a major way historically in the Christian-driven movement against slavery. Slavery is a norm and accepted in the New Testament, yet the teachings of Christ and Paul on the equality of all before God had to have an impact on the heinous practice of buying and selling people. It's now seen as contrary to Christian belief.

Ellen White was a commonsense enthusiast. "We are to be guided by true theology and common sense," she admonished (*Counsels to Parents*,

Teachers, and Students, page 257). And for a truly modern edge, she has advice for those engaged in the worship wars: "Common sense is an excellent thing in the worship of the Lord" (*Testimonies for the Church*, Vol 4, page 71). That's applicable to both sides of the argument.

Commonsense focuses more on principles than specifics, because specifics can change. Commonsense allows us to adjust to situations, but remains true to basic biblical belief. For instance, commonsense theology understands the eternal principles of the Sabbath and Sabbath-keeping, but adjusts itself to the situation in the keeping of the Sabbath.

Ellen White said it well: "God wants us all to have common sense, and He wants us to reason from common sense. Circumstances alter conditions. Circumstances change the relation of things" (*Selected Messages*, Book 3, page 217).

The apostle Paul had Jesus' promise concerning snakebite fulfilled on the island of Malta (Acts 28). Paul carried an armful of sticks for the fire without realising he also carried a snake. When the snake bit him, the reaction from those with him was such that it must have been a poisonous snake—they waited for him to swell up or drop dead. When he didn't, they thought he must be a god.

This accident is in quite a different category to that of deliberately handling snakes as a test of faith. That test is like asking God to perform some kind of magic trick to save the believer from being bitten or, if bitten, to save their life. It would be far better not to test the Lord.

Spencer Evans and his supporters need to add a touch of commonsense to their theology. As do we.

THE CHALLENGE
OF "PRESENT TRUTH"

One of the strengths of the Adventist Church has been its refusal to formulate a creed. Historically, it has taken a position known as "present truth." This concept is first found in Peter when he wrote that believers were to "be established in the present truth" (2 Peter 1:12, KJV).

Present Truth became the title of two Adventist magazines, the first (1849-50) combined with another and is now the *Adventist Review*. The second, a semimonthly, ran from 1917 to 1955.

Our pioneers linked present truth with the three angels' messages of Revelation 14. Joseph Bates saw present truth in the shut door (the door of mercy being shut for those who rejected the Jesus-is-coming-in-1844 "truth") and the Sabbath.

James White, in the first issue of *Present Truth* (July 1849), wrote that the church has always had a present truth. "The present truth now, is that which shows present duty, and the right position for us, who are about to witness the time of trouble, such as never was."

Ellen White added: "The doctrines we hold today are present truth"; and, later, "The truth for this time embraces the whole gospel" (*Testimonies for the Church*, Vol 2, page 355; and Vol 6, page 291).

Fast-forward to 1980, the last time the General Conference in session voted on the full document of the church's fundamental beliefs. Perhaps the most important statement isn't found in the 27 fundamentals themselves, but in the preamble (which came from a delegate, from the floor of the meeting).

The preamble indicates that we have no creed but the Bible, and hold "certain fundamental beliefs." "Revision of these statements may be expected at a General Conference session when the church is led by the Holy Spirit to a fuller understanding of Bible truth or finds better language in which to express the teachings of God's Holy Word."

Of the pioneers, Ellen White was strongest on the need for "thorough and continuous searching of the Scriptures for greater light" (see *Testimonies for the Church*, Vol 5, pages 706-8). She argued that if the church is growing in grace, it will constantly find "new light and beauty in [the Bible's] sacred truths." She expected disagreement in the process. Her greater fear was that the church would become "conservative and seek to avoid discussion" or hold to tradition and "worship they know not what."

The concept of present truth creates challenges on several fronts:
- We shouldn't expect core truths to change. Our understanding may, but the basics won't—salvation through Jesus Christ is a core truth; the Sabbath is a core truth and so on. They won't change, but our

understanding of them should deepen. We may find better ways of explaining them. You'll find evidence of this in the 1980 fundamentals statement when compared to earlier statements.
- We should expect society, compassion and other influences to force us to pursue further biblical understanding in a variety of areas. In recent times the church has considered the role of women, ecology, homosexuality and suicide. With asylum seekers a growing world problem, we could expect a "stranger-within-your-gates" discussion.
- If the concept of present truth means a progression of understanding, it is also a warning that, like Joseph Bates's claim that the shut door was present truth, some things must be let go.

Occasionally, some urge us to go back to selected teachings of the pioneers—the anti-trinitarian teaching of some pioneers is currently in the spotlight. But do we deny present truth when we argue a case from 150 years ago, from 100 years ago or even 50 years ago? Put another way, Do we deny God's leading since then? We may not, but the question must be asked.

Present truth has a personal responsibility—on two fronts: Do we read our Bibles to confirm what we believe or do we read them to see what God is saying? In the truest sense, those who accept the concept of present truth will be seekers and not merely revisers.

And, if we discover a new truth, are we willing to submit to others? We are called to be loyal to His body, with the biblical example of the Jerusalem council of how these matters should be handled. Notice: "Paul and Barnabas were sent to Jerusalem, accompanied by some local believers, to talk to the apostles and elders about this question" (Acts 15:2, NLT).

The challenge of the concept of present truth is that it places responsibility on us and our church to keep studying, to keep learning and to be gracious with those who may differ in their understanding. From study and discussion within the body of Christ we remain in present truth. There continues to be strength in not having a creed.

WHEN THEOLOGY GOES POP

The Prayer of Jabez was a bestseller for Bruce Wilkinson. The book's basic premise is that if you use the formula for prayer that Jabez used (found in 1 Chronicles 4:9, 10), you will find security and growth in your life path.

To be fair, it is a good read, and it does challenge the reader to be open to God's leading. But it is another example, if we needed one, of pop theology. That is, theology that mines a popular vein rather than staying true to strict biblical teaching.

The prayer itself is just one verse long and wasn't intended as a prayer formula. To understand the Bible's teaching on prayer, you need to compare other passages, including the Lord's Prayer.

What is more concerning, though, is the pop theology infiltrating our church—Sabbath school classes and, sometimes, even our pulpits. It can occur as with Wilkinson's book or, perhaps, when someone becomes enthusiastic about a prophetic interpretation they see is being fulfilled.

Then there's that other kind of interpretation where a thought has "popped" into a person's head as they read a passage, to be shared as if it were part of Bible teaching.

You don't have to be a theologian

You don't have to be a theologian to understand the Bible. But you do have to understand that there are certain basic rules to discover true biblical teaching. And it's as simple as asking the kinds of questions a journalist would ask: Who? What? Where? When? Why? How?

Who? Who wrote the message? To whom was it written?

What? What is the message? And what is the whole message, not just the portion that interests me?

Where? Where are these people—the writer and the recipients? What are their circumstances?

When? When was the text first written? Importantly, was it before or after the time of Jesus?

Why? Why was this message important for the original readers or hearers?

How? How does the message fit with the teaching found in the rest of the Bible? How does it help us understand the overall teaching of the Bible? And then, how does it fit my circumstance?

To answer some of those questions you will need study aids, but they're readily available. Besides, with computers, one CD-ROM can give a library of resources and translations.

Answering these questions helps us to understand the text. Also needed is the spiritual preparedness to study the text—prayer and openness to the Spirit's leading.

Lessons from a Latin teacher

Knowledge of Bible teachings doesn't necessarily indicate an understanding of how to study the Bible. Bible doctrines are important, but they can be learned by rote for a ready answer. We fail new believers and our children if we simply teach them Bible doctrines without teaching *how* to study the Bible for themselves.

When I was in high school I studied Latin—for a few weeks. I lasted until my Latin teacher suggested I do geography. But, more than three decades later, I still remember some of the vocabulary. I can tell you the correct Latin word for "spear" (*hasta*), but I don't know how to place it in a sentence, not even a one-word sentence!

In the same way it is possible to give a learned answer to the what-happens-when-you-die? question without knowing the Bible. We need to know the answer to the question, but also how to discover the answer.

Age of shifting truth

One of the most notable beliefs in our current age is that truth is relative and is found within ourselves. Pop theology fits well into this scene, for it's theology that can be made to fit popular teaching or our feelings within.

Yes, there is a valid, devotional use of the Bible, where it's read for the purpose of asking What is the text saying to *me*? The Lord can take such an approach and use it to enrich our lives—it's obvious, for instance, that the prayer of Jabez has enriched Wilkinson's life, but that doesn't mean he's giving the complete biblical message.

The Bible is God-breathed. It is designed to teach, rebuke, correct and train in righteousness. And it is to equip us for good works (see 2 Timothy 3:16, 17). We must take it seriously.

Pop theology tends to be the kind of theology that fits us, rather than us fitting with what the Word says. That's always dangerous.

LET'S NOT
GET TRIGGER HAPPY

"I waited all Tuesday [October 22, 1844] and dear Jesus did not come—I waited all the forenoon of Wednesday, and was well in body as I ever was, but after 12 o'clock I began to feel faint, and before dark I needed someone to help me up to my chamber. . . . I lay prostrate for two days without any pain—sick with disappointment."*

Henry Emmons's experience is a safeguard for Seventh-day Adventists as we draw near to the year 2000. We know better than to set a date for the return of Jesus.

Yet it is tempting to set a date when things seem to be falling into place because it captures people's attention, and it helps them focus on the importance of being God's person. However, no matter how fervent you may be, there's nothing like a failed prediction to dampen enthusiasm.

The impact is twofold. First, it discredits the movement—and God. Listen: "The world still hangs fire. The old planet is still on track, notwithstanding the efforts to 'stop 'er.' The 'believers' in this city, after being up a few nights watching and making noises like serenading tom cats, have now gone to bed and concluded to take a snooze. We hope they will wake up rational beings!" (*The Cleveland Plain Dealer*, October 30, 1884.)

Second, it shatters the faith of the believer. "Our fondest hopes and expectations were blasted, and such a spirit of weeping came over us as I never experienced before . . ." wrote Hiram Edson. "We wept and wept till the day dawn. . . . If this has proved a failure, what was the rest of my Christian experience worth? Has the Bible proved a failure? Is there no God—no heaven—no golden home city—no paradise? Is all this but a cunningly devised fable?"

The Bible is plain. Jesus gave the warning: "No-one knows about that day or hour, not even the angels in heaven . . ." (Matthew 24:36).

Lesson learned? Well, maybe.

Some Seventh-day Adventists are replacing date setting with pseudo date setting—"triggers." It goes something like this: This will trigger that, will trigger this other thing, will trigger something else and presto!—the Lord is here.

A current trigger** is the millennium bug, but it has been—can be— a war in the Middle East, a piece of religious legislation or a papal encyclical. Throw in some speculation and a conspiracy theory or two and you can end up with strong "evidence."

That we should be aware of what is happening about us is the point of Matthew 24. "When you see all these things [the signs Jesus has been talking about], you know that it is near, right at the door" (verse 33). We need to be aware of trends, of the chaos, of the disasters that point to His return. We need to understand the return is imminent.

But note Jesus' warning: "Be ready, because the Son of Man will come at an hour when you do not expect him" (Matthew 24:44). When we try to box God into our dates and times, or within the triggers we devise, He's likely to act like a jack-in-a-box—jumping out at the most unexpected time.

More than half of Jesus' sermon from the Mount of Olives (Matthew 24 and 25) is about living in waiting. The lessons are in the parables (Matthew 24:45–25:46):

- The faithful and wise servant remains faithful while the master is away, even if the master is away longer than expected.
- None of the 10 girls stays awake during the waiting time (for the bridegroom), but five are caught out by the delay. The lesson is plain, "Keep watch, because you do not know the day or hour" (Matthew 25:13).
- The master gives his servants talents to care for while he goes on a

journey. God, the giver of all good gifts, gives His servants gifts to care for. He asks us to be good stewards of the life, the abilities and the spiritual gifts He has given until He returns.
- Jesus gives a final warning in the parable of the sheep and goats: judgment is coming and it will be real. There's a reminder in the story of how we are to represent Jesus while we wait.

Our main task is not to know when Jesus is coming (He says that's impossible, anyway); it's to be ready. Being ready has nothing to do with attempts at second-guessing God; it has everything to do with remaining faithful to Him.

*Non-biblical quotations from George R Knight, *Millennial Fever*, Pacific Press, Boise, Idaho, 1993.

**Written June 5, 1999.

THE BEAST, BAR CODES
AND BILL GATES

Bill Gates is the antichrist. Sorry, could be the antichrist. According to one source, "[I] wouldn't be surprised if Bill Gates was the antichrist. After all, it was already foretold in the Bible that someone powerful would rise up and lead the world to destruction."

And the worldwide web (www), almost under his control, bears the sign of the beast. How can we tell? W W W can also be written as VI VI VI says this source, which, as any eight-year-old can tell you, is 666.

Buying and selling? Isn't everything moving toward Internet sales? If Gates gains total control of the Internet, he'll control sales. Marked in the forehead or hand? Computer monitors are for the forehead; the computer mouse is for the hand.

"What if WWW is 666? Or Bill Gates be the beast? What will you do? It bears thinking about!"

Yes, it bears thinking about—for half a nanosecond. And so many theories concerning the mark of the beast deserve no more attention.

Every bar code has three sixes on it, right? ("If you don't believe it, get a bar code and look at it," I'm told.) Well, it isn't true, but the thought catches your attention. And bar codes could be placed on your forehead or hand (some say invisible bar codes). If you go through a checkout without the bar code, you won't be able to buy.

Several watch-for-the-end-time groups became quite excited when England's BBC reported that, as part of an experiment, a scientist had a silicon chip temporarily implanted in his arm in August last year. A computer was able to keep track of the device—and the scientist. (This isn't altogether new; computer-chip implants have been available for animals for some time.)

According to some, this device works best in the forehead or the hand, where body temperature is the most desirable. As an afterthought, they add that when the lithium batteries break down in the implants, the user will come out in the terrible sores of Revelation 17:11.

Enough!

Let's be biblical

These kinds of interpretations may bring a tingle of anticipation, but they're neither faithful to the biblical text nor to its proper exegesis. They especially fail to notice the context.

In both places where the mark of the beast is mentioned (Revelation 13:16-18 and 14:9-11), it's in a setting of highly symbolic imagery. Beasts are paraded, an image set up, there's a call to worship the beast, Babylon is fallen. You aren't meant to think of literal beasts or a literal Babylon, but of powers political and ecclesiastical.

We fail to be true to the context and symbolic intent of the passage if we suddenly switch to tattoos or bar codes—literal marks on the hands and foreheads. And, for Adventists, there's nothing new in this thought. Back in 1957 the *SDA Bible Commentary* noted, "Adventist interpreters understand this mark to be not a literal brand, but some sign of allegiance that identifies the bearer as loyal to the power represented by the beast" (on Revelation 13:16).

The commentary then notes that the controversy of the time will focus on the law of God, "and particularly on the fourth commandment."

The big issue of the Revelation 13 and 14 passages is loyalty to God in the end-times. The three angels' messages of chapter 14 focus on worship—worship to the One who provides the eternal gospel; who is the judge and creator; and who calls for faithfulness and obedience. He calls for loyalty.

The other option is worship to the beast and his image, and to be marked by the beast. The Greek word used here for "mark," *charagma*, was commonly used for an object, or a slave marked to designate the owner. That helps make sense of the text that says those who worship the beast or his image will receive the "mark of his name" (Revelation 14:11).

The "mark of his name" shows that the biblical emphasis is on the name of the beast, not the number. The same emphasis appears in Revelation 13:17 where the number is "the number of his name." Two verses later, those marked with the name of the beast are contrasted with the 144,000 who have the name of the Father on their foreheads.

The mark of the beast is about ownership and loyalty to the owner. Who owns you? is the question.

Let's not lose sight of the real issue in speculation about bar codes, computer chips and Bill Gates.

VANISHING HITCHHIKERS
AND SIGNS OF HELL

A man drives along a lonely stretch of road at night. He sees a hitchhiker and stops to pick him up. As they drive and talk, the man becomes impressed that there's something about the hitchhiker—a presence.

The hitchhiker turns the conversation to the Second Coming. "It's happening soon," he says. "Be ready!" Message given, the hitchhiker disappears.

Another time, another place. A motorist is stranded by the side of the road, so a businessman offers him a ride to town. As they talk, the businessman is intrigued by what the motorist is saying—and again, there's that sense of presence. The topic turns to the Second Coming.

"The Lord is coming back soon!" says the motorist—and he disappears. Somewhat shaken, the businessman reports the incident to the police.

"Normally we wouldn't believe you," the police officer says, "but you're the fifth caller today telling us of the same experience."

Unbelievable! Warnings from angelic beings? No, just unbelievable.

As much as these stories might stir the hearts of those awaiting the Advent; as much as the warning of the nearness of the Advent may be needed, the stories aren't true. Versions of these stories have been doing the rounds for years. Every now and again they resurface and are passed on.

A few years ago Brian Finn, from *Challenge Weekly* in New Zealand, attempted to follow up about 40 such reports. He found no-one who had actually experienced a hitchhiker incident. And none of the police departments mentioned in the stories had received reports of vanishing hitchhikers.

And that, *The Vanishing Hitchhiker*, is what Jan Brunvand entitled one of his books on urban myths. Apparently, versions of the vanishing hitchhiker go back to the 1800s. What began as a ghost story gained Christian overtones as it developed (ghosts still sometimes feature), until it has become the most widely spread Christian urban myth.

We want to believe, and sometimes that desire stops us asking the right questions—in this case, who? where? and when? and how do I contact this person?

Claims and conspiracy theories bedevil Christianity.

From the damaging: When US company Proctor and Gamble was accused of supporting satanism with its profits and company logo, it cost the company more than $US10 million dollars to clear its name and replace its 100-year-old logo. The claim was false and could be checked—few bothered.

To the intriguing: What *did* happen to that Bible code theory that was popular a few years back?

To the silly: The year 1998, was the devil's year. The number of the year

13

is 999 (add the 1 to the 8 to make the third 9), which, when inverted, makes 666—the number of the beast.

My personal favourite is the story of a group of scientists in Russia who stopped digging a deep hole when workmen said they heard voices. The story was picked up by some Christian newsletters and magazines, several with inferences that hell had been found. It stopped when a journalist put up his hand and confessed he'd made up the story.

Be warned! There is a danger of following "cunningly devised fables" (2 Peter 1:16, KJV). Claims need to be checked, questions need to be asked, the evidence needs to be tested—no matter how fervent, sincere or believable the claim or those making the claims. Fervency and sincerity may actually blind an individual to reality. (Do we believe those who claim to have been taken by aliens on the basis of their fervency or sincerity?)

Christianity is a faith religion, but it isn't blind faith. The greatest claim of Christianity is the resurrection of Jesus. Agnostics and atheists understand that if they can disprove the Resurrection, Christianity falls.

Paul understood that: "If Christ has not been raised, your faith is futile . . ." (1 Corinthians 15:17). But he defends the reality of the Resurrection in 1 Corinthians 15 by virtually saying, "If you don't believe me, there are more than 500 witnesses who have seen the risen Jesus—ask them." And most of these witnesses lived only a three-day journey away from Corinth (by sea). It wasn't difficult for Paul's claim to be checked.

Those witnesses and the empty tomb are firm evidences for belief in the Resurrection. God provides solid support for the step of faith He asks us to take. Fairness and accuracy demand the same kind of evidence from claims supposed to support the faith.

EINSTEIN AND TAKING
TRUTH TO THE LIMIT

You'll find Albert Einstein's brain preserved in a jar in a laboratory somewhere in Missouri, USA. After his death in 1955, when he had no more use for it, it was decided his brain needed checking to see if there were any physical differences between his brain and a normal one. Maybe, they thought, there was a simple, physical explanation for him being one of the foremost scientific minds of this century.

Disappointment. His brain, apparently, is rather ordinary.

One time, the story goes, he was showing a visitor around the Institute for Advanced Studies at Princeton University when the guest asked to see Einstein's laboratory. Einstein smiled and pointed to his head.

Out of this laboratory came $E=mc^2$—a truth that opened up a new world of scientific endeavour. (If it isn't a truth and you can prove it, you'll probably have your face on T-shirts 50 years after your death.)

His theories of relativity gave a greater, and a popular, appreciation of our universe and brought significant scientific discoveries that have changed the face of the world.

The truth was taken beyond theoretical bounds. Where truth belongs. All truth. Especially biblical truth.

You can approach the Bible as if the truths there were part of a general knowledge quest. It's always handy, for instance, to have an answer ready in case you're ever asked, "Who was the father of Mahalaleel?" (No, I'm not against general knowledge of the Bible, but there needs to be more.)

Some seem to approach Bible truth in that way. "Yes, I know the truth about the Sabbath," they say. "I've got that one right. And the truth about the state of the dead. And I've got my prophetic mathematics right—I even know how to cross the BC–AD date line in the 490 days/years prophecy."

If it goes no further than this, it's academic. Theoretical. And condemned. By Jesus.

Note His anger in Matthew 23 as He publicly confronts the teachers of the law and the Pharisees. There's no doubt they know the truth, and they're following it—in a sense. They're Sabbath-keepers, they're waiting for the Messiah, they're tithe-payers—but something is missing.

Jesus condemned them for living out the truth on a literal, minimalist level. They could say, "I've never murdered" or "I've never stolen." But Jesus, in the Sermon on the Mount, asked, "Have you ever hated someone? Ever been envious?" He's attempting to lift them to a higher level.

Peter explains the impact of truth best: "Now that you have purified yourselves by obeying the truth so that you have sincere love for your brothers, love one another deeply, from the heart" (1 Peter 1:22).

This makes sense only if we understand that biblical truth is not information, but living truth. And that living truth is centred in the One who said, "I am . . . the truth" (John 14:6). As we look at the life of Jesus, we see that His perfect obedience to the truth resulted in deep love and compassion for all. He's the example.

See Him with the children rejected by the disciples. See Him with the woman at the well. See Him treating with respect the woman caught in adultery. See Him touching the untouchables. See His strength as He tackles religious and moral wrongs. See Him asking for forgiveness for those who nailed Him to the cross.

What an example!

We followers of Truth, and we students of truth, are to do likewise. And it's to begin among ourselves. Listen: "A new command I give you: Love one another. As I have loved you, so you must love one another. By this all men will know that you are my disciples, if you love one another" (John 13:34, 35).

Living the truth with love is more convincing than preaching the truth. Both are necessary, but living the truth with love has the greater impact.

You don't have to be an Einstein to work out that this could be more difficult than attempting to understand $E=mc^2$.

FROM FEAR
TO GLORY

You've known fear. I have. That stomach-wrenching, heart-pumping, mind-throttling fear with my car spinning wildly out of control. That stab of fear when answering the phone to hear, "I've got some bad news . . ." That harrowing, exhausting fear when a family member is long overdue, with no word.

"Fear God . . . ," says the first angel of Revelation 14.

Wait! Isn't this the same angel who brings eternal good news (the gospel)? Having a "painful feeling of impending danger" (a *Macquarie Dictionary* definition of fear) every time we think of God doesn't sound like good news to me. There must be another definition to the word *fear*.

And there is: "reverential awe, esp. towards God," adds *The Macquarie Dictionary*. You don't have to understand Greek (*phobeo*, according to the *Seventh-day Adventist Bible Commentary*, has the same meanings as *fear*) to know what the angel is saying.

This awe is much more than Lewis Lapham (in *Harper's*) suggests: "Proper show of respect when addressing persons blessed with annual incomes in excess of $500,000." (No, Lapham wasn't serious.)

Awe may cause a quickening of the heart or a thrill down the spine—maybe that's why it's related to fear.

You've known awe. I have. A breathtaking sunrise. Holding a newborn baby—ours. Discovering God's plan for my life. Awesome.

Reverential awe? What else can you have toward God when you realise and accept what He has done? The three angels' messages of Revelation 14 are founded in the gospel. The gospel tells us that Jesus left heaven to suffer hell for us. Living the life we couldn't, He died the death we should have to give us new life we don't deserve. This new life gives meaning for the present and the promise of life eternal for the future. As if that weren't enough, He adopts us into His family; His father is our Father.

Any conditions?

Sure—belief and acceptance. (Have you taken the time to meditate on John 3:16 lately?) That means believing Jesus died for you, and accepting the gift of life He offers and that it is yours. Absolutely awesome!

For the nonbeliever, this doesn't make sense.

We see the evidence of this in society. Even though, in Australia and New Zealand, we call ourselves Christian nations, there is often less respect for Christianity than for other religions. And so often God is relegated to an irrelevance trotted out for weddings or funerals; a handy curse word; or a joke in a stand-up comic's routine.

Not that this is a new problem. Paul writes of those who don't believe as ones who saw his message as a "stumbling block" and "foolishness, " a joke, if you like. But the believers "whom God has called . . . [see] Christ the power of God and the wisdom of God" (1 Corinthians 1:24).

Yet even the believer can lose sight of the awesomeness of God. Yes, there is a case and a place for the Abba (Father) God, for the God who is a mate who sticks through thick and thin, and for the God who comforts in the valley of the shadow. But they represent only one dimension of God. He is also the Creator God, the Saviour God, the omnipotent, omniscient, omnipresent God.

This is the God who said to Moses, "I will show you my glory, but first I will hide you in the cleft in a rock, then I will cover your face until I pass by. When I've passed by, I will allow you to see just a part of me— for otherwise you will die."

The power of God is awesome. As is His love. For His love allows us to call Him Father and Friend.

Even as we who believe grapple with understanding the fullness and breadth of God there are moments when, in His presence, we're caught in absolute awe of Him. This is how it should be.

"Fear God and give him glory," says the first angel. The glory, honour, praise and worship He deserves.

"Blessed is the man who fears the Lord . . ." (Psalm 112:1).

"The fear [awe] of the Lord is the beginning of wisdom . . ." (Proverbs 9:10).

A PLUMBER
GOES A-PLUMBING

Not too many Adventists fix plumbing on Sabbath afternoons. And when I read the story, it captured my attention, because it raised all sorts of issues about Sabbath-keeping.

It was only a brief story, about one page in length, from a book I'd borrowed for some holiday reading (Richard M Davidson, *A Love Song for the Sabbath*, Review and Herald).

A new Adventist, a plumber by trade, moved into a community in the southern part of the United States. The church was small and Adventists really had little impact in the community. In fact, the pastor had run an evangelistic program in the town about the time the new Adventist arrived and no-one, except church members, attended.

The plumber was enthusiastic about his faith, but he didn't have the voice to participate in the church's singing group, and he didn't feel he had the knowledge to give Bible studies.

On Sabbaths he attended Sabbath school and church. But every Sabbath afternoon he loaded his plumber's tools into the back of his pick-up truck and drove around town, or into the country, where he felt he could find people who were "oppressed." The oppressed he defined as the poor, the widows, the disabled and so on.

He would approach them and ask if they had any plumbing in their houses that needed fixing. When the job was finished and he was asked how much he charged, he would say, "No charge! This is God's gift to you on His holy Sabbath."

With that he would drive off.

I felt uncomfortable with the story. I almost felt like checking to see if Adventist Book Centres (ABCs) had the audacity to still stock the book; or writing to Review and Herald to question the wisdom of publishing the story. Something within said that there must be at least a dozen verses in the Bible that say: "Thou shalt not plumb on Sabbaths."

At least *the* commandments say, "On it [the Sabbath] you shall not do any work . . ." (Exodus 20:9).

I feel comfortable with the helping vocations—nursing, for instance—doing their helping, and with almost any work being done on the Sabbath under emergency situations. But plumbing? Does the fact that he takes no money make a difference? Does that mean he's performing a helping ministry?

If he were a member of your church, would you be tempted to take him before the church board for some kind of disciplinary measures? Would he be an embarrassment? Would you be happy with the way he represented your church and the Sabbath? Would you ask the pastor to have a quiet chat with him?

If we don't have this kind of reaction, should we consider joining him and organise bands of church members who go out lawn mowing, house painting and conducting repairs for the needy on Sabbath afternoons? Is this a natural extension and progression from things such as hospital visitation, soup kitchens and street witnessing?

The downside, for the plumber, is the fact that he's doing what he does any other day of the week. The Sabbath becomes just another day where he is up to his elbows in a grease trap—or worse. I guess he would say that his attitude toward his work is different on the Sabbath.

In fairness to him we ought to ask another question: Who is the one who commits the greater sin, the person who spends every Sabbath afternoon catching up on sleep or the plumber who spends every Sabbath afternoon helping the needy?

I didn't contact the ABC or Review and Herald because there was one part of the story that really did make me think. A year after the plumber arrived in town, the pastor ran another evangelistic program in the local church. This time the church had standing room only. People turned up eager to learn about the plumber's God and His Sabbath.

If they turned up to your church, what would you tell them about Sabbath-keeping?

KEEPING THE THEOLOGY
SIMPLE

Jesus understood the theology, but He kept it simple. Childlike simple. "It's like this," He would say, and tell a story: A farmer went to sow . . . ; A merchant searched for a pearl . . . ; A king had a feast. . . .

And He taught through His encounters with people. His theology was practical. It changed lives—lives like Mary's. Remember how she responded? With the expensive perfume?

The perfume came from the root of the plant *Nardostachys jatamansi*. The plant was found only to the north of India, high enough up in the Himalayas that lack of oxygen made you light-headed. In ancient times it was both difficult to find and difficult to transport. And then it went through a dozen middlemen and another dozen or so tax booths. Each added cost to the final product.

Mixed with a base, often olive oil, it was prized as both a medicine and a perfume. Only the wealthy could afford it, so it was often used as a gift for kings and emperors.

Yet Mary anointed the feet of Jesus with it. The cost? Judas reckoned, out loud, that it would have paid a wage for a year.

Absolute extravagance!

No wonder there were murmurs among the guests at the feast. They didn't need much persuasion to agree with Judas that it could have been sold for money for the poor.

But wait! "Why are you bothering this woman?" asked Jesus. "She has done a beautiful thing to me" (Matthew 26:10).

Mary was driven by love to make this "beautiful" gesture. She was willing to suffer ridicule and embarrassment to demonstrate her feelings for her Lord, her Master.

Not that this act gave her any bonus points in her quest for heaven. Jesus tells her that her act doesn't give her any credit for salvation, for He says, "Your faith has saved you; go in peace" (Luke 7:50). Here He teaches about salvation, and the theology is simple.

Faith is the basis of salvation. Christianity is a faith religion, for nothing saves us outside the grace and works of God. There's nothing we can *do* that will make us acceptable to God. The songwriter said it well: "Nothing in my hand I bring;/ Simply to Thy cross I cling."

And what then? Listen: "You were once darkness, but now you are light in the Lord. Live as children of light" (Ephesians 5:8).

And again: "We do not earn salvation by our obedience; for salvation is the free gift of God, to be received by faith. But obedience is the fruit of faith" (*Steps to Christ*, page 61).

We don't talk much about obedience. It's as if there's a fear that we might be trying to win favour with God (legalism). Of course some say that having been made right with God through faith is all that's needed—obedience and good works have no meaning (antinomianism).

Then there are the weird. Rasputin the mad Russian monk developed a theology that he should sin more, for the more he sinned, the more God could demonstrate His grace and saving power.

But the Christian life is an obedient life. Obedience is not legalism.

Obedience is not a sin.

The greatest champion of salvation *by faith*, the apostle Paul, always emphasised Christian living. Read his letters and you'll discover he assumed and sometimes demanded an obedient life from Christians.

The quest for the obedient life should cause us to pause and ask specifics: How do I relate to the people around me? Am I using my time in the best possible way? Am I generous with my money? Are *things* too high on my priority list? How does my Sabbath-keeping rate? Am I careful enough about what I drink and eat?

And if that seems like a burden, we need to remember that the obedient life is one focused on living for God, not for ourselves. Because we are His and part of His family (see John 1:12), we'll want to be like our Father.

Our obedience becomes a thank offering for the goodness of God to us. Our obedience is a gift to God.

Dare we be as extravagant as Mary with her gift? How often have we caused the Lord to say, "He/she has done a beautiful thing to Me"?

You can make the theology as complex as you like—some seem to need it that way. But once you blow away the verbiage, Christianity comes back to a very simple formula: Trust and obey. There's just no other way.

When first published, this was the second of two parts. "Keeping the Theology Simple—1" was memorable for two reasons: it was my shortest editorial; and the title was longer than the editorial. It consisted of three words: "Trust and obey."

CHURCH WAS SIMPLE
. . . WHEN?

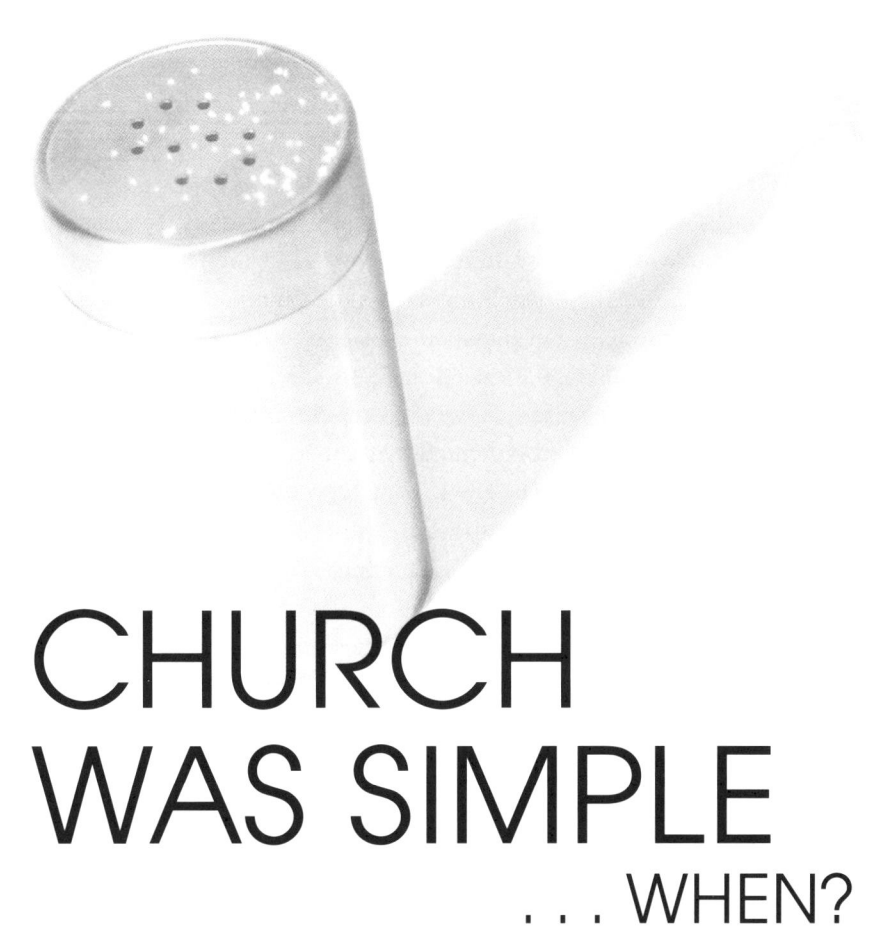

CHURCH WAS SIMPLE
. . . WHEN?

Life through nostalgia-tinted glasses tends to be in warm tones. In slow motion sometimes. Life was just better back then. Life made more sense. Life was simpler.

For those of us who grew up Adventist, it's the church of the earlier days—of our childhood—that tends to have that soft-focus, endless summer look and feel about it. Church was simpler then. Wasn't it?

Beginnings . . . simple?

Sometimes we forget that an international organisation, such as our church, began with a few scattered believers in a limited area of the United States. Sure, they had a message and a mission, and they had daring and commitment. But they had little else.

The miracle is that they survived and attracted others to the cause. They had limited resources. They were shunned by mainstream Adventists. Worse, they were ridiculed by their society for preaching and believing Jesus would return in 1844. They grew out of a failed prophecy.

They were a nothing group that didn't believe in organising themselves. Adventist George Storrs summed that attitude up well early in 1844 in the *Midnight Cry*: "No church can be organised by man's invention but that it becomes Babylon *the moment it is organised*."

Only as others joined them did they begin to ordain ministers and organise themselves in a way that would bring greater unity of purpose and stronger growth. Life was not simple then.

Back in my day . . . simple?

My memories of being a teenager in the Adventist Church in the 1960s are warm. The church of that era in the South Pacific was riding high on success. It was growing at an unprecedented rate. It was a comfortable place to be. Some even reckoned you could tell who was Adventist simply by looking at them. We were proud, mostly, of who we were.

But these were the days of revolution outside. Authority was being challenged, as was Christian orthodoxy. The pill heralded a sexual revolution and teens began to dictate popular music and culture.

Except for the challenges to Christianity, these issues were rarely addressed in a meaningful way. Our success meant they didn't have to be addressed. We knew we were right and we could see what God was doing! Besides, the mellow sounds of the King's Heralds, the Heritage Singers and Tennessee Ernie Ford coming from our radiograms muffled what was happening outside.

Robert Ellwood, in *The Sixties Spiritual Awakening*, suggests the 1960s brought a transition from modern to postmodern times, creating endless "ripples of private opinions in pluralistic puddles." At the time, though, few recognised how well cocooned the church was from the realities of the day. Or how those pluralistic puddles would impact on the church later.

Today . . . simple?

The church of today is large, worldwide, at some 13 million members. Its complexities are visible. In any congregation there can be a variety of theological opinions. It is in danger of becoming an institutionalised church run by committees that wet-blanket creativity. There's the threat of the church being controlled by budgets instead of ministry.

Some congregations appear as if their life has been sucked out of them. Some have an attractive and involving vibrancy. Some are traditional, some are otherwise. Some meet in large church buildings, some in people's homes.

The church of today is anything but simple.

So . . . ?

Life, and church, is never as simple as we would want. However, there is a missing element in these descriptions of church past and present that is an essential: God!

From a human perspective the Adventist movement should have disintegrated before it began. After the 1844 disappointment there should have been no-one left to form the Seventh-day Adventist Church. But God already had the people and the plan in mind.

In every era of the Christian church's history and our church's history you find human failings and weaknesses. They're easy to find. If you fail to also see God at work, though, you miss the full picture.

During the three periods mentioned you will find God's people fulfilling His will. They're promoting His kingdom. They're changing the world—for Him.

There's no question that we can learn from the past. We can build on the foundation laid by those before us. At the same time we need to focus on the One who guides the present and is our future.

The church is a group of people commissioned to preach a risen and saving Lord. We await and proclaim His return. After the Coming, then church will be simple.

WHY BOTHER
WITH CHURCH?

At its best, church is a place of fellowship, inspiration and involving worship. At its worst it can be destructive. Stating the obvious, church is such a human place. It's so human that, at times, it's difficult to find the divine presence.

People can be hurt in church. The ideal is the Christlikeness that Christ's followers want to achieve. But let's admit it, you also find hypocrisy, the tendency to gossip, the strong feelings over church issues and the unbending attitude some adopt.

If salvation is offered personally and individually through Jesus Christ, and the church gives me pain, why bother with it? Surely I would do better travelling alone than risking the kind of injury I could get from fellow Christians.

Wrong, and for three reasons:

Jesus' response

Imagine if Jesus set up a complaints booth at church. What would you say?

"I don't like church because of the hypocritical attitude I find here!"

"Hmmm-mmm," He says.

"The preaching's just not up to scratch!"

"Hmmm-mm."

"If only You knew what one of the members said about me."

"Yes, I know." And He does.

"Nobody cares. Nobody talks to me."

"Hmmm-mmm."

He's patient. He listens to this and more. He then says, "I've heard what you've said, but I don't see the problem."

What . . .?

"Look at Me!"

When you do, you discover something from the example Jesus set. He worshipped with those He called hypocrites in the Jerusalem temple. Jesus was belittled by priests, baited by religious lawyers and arrested by religious police—people He worshipped with.

Religious leaders with political intent placed Him on the cross. Roman soldiers drove the nails through His flesh and bones, but He was led to His death with the chants of religious people—fellow church members—calling for His crucifixion.

Would Jesus go to church? It's a nonsense question. Of course He would. And does. He's where His people are; that's a promise. He's used to being in church with worse than anything we've ever encountered.

The power of 11

Yes, there is the power of one, but there's more power in the many. Jesus chose 12 disciples, not one. Losing one, the 11 changed the world. Their success came not in establishing individual agents across the empire, but church communities.

Every Christian has a God-given responsibility to give salt-flavour to their part of the world, to add light to their corner. But there's far greater strength in combining the resources and spiritual gifts that are part of any Christian community. In fellowship, worship and witness, the church becomes greater than individual points of light; it becomes a beacon in a dark world.

What would the apostles say?

Richard Rice writes of the often-asked question (in *Believing, Behaving, Belonging*), "'Can I be a Christian without joining the church? Isn't it enough for me to accept Jesus as my Saviour and have a strong relationship with Him?' What would the apostles say?"

He suggests they wouldn't understand the question. "As Paul describes it, the experience of becoming a Christian involves becoming part of the community that Jesus established." Paul says, "You are the body of Christ, and each one of you is a part of it" (1 Corinthians 12:27).

For John, the mark of being a follower of Jesus is to love fellow disciples (see John 15:12). "What you are, they [Paul and John] assert, is more fundamental and more important than anything you can be by yourself." Participating in the community life is "not a consequence of salvation; it is an indispensable part of the experience."

There's a truth here that may be difficult for us who live in an individualistic society where "I" is more important than "you," and "they" barely rate on our awareness scale. Not only is it important that we, as members of the body of Christ, fellowship and worship together, but we are to reflect the love of Christ for each other.

Love is what should make church different to any other organisation, and it's Jesus' expectation (see John 13:35). Somehow we need to become like stones being polished in a drum so that, as we tumble against each other, the sharp edges are smoothed and we each become a thing of beauty. For Him.

In the midst of the humanness of church—the criticism, the hypocrisy and intolerance—how do we lift ourselves out of the mire? Jesus answers that it's about focus.

He says, again, "Look at Me!"

CONSUMING
PASSIONS

The Beatles arrived in Australia in the 1960s to a stunning welcome. For example, in Adelaide, an estimated third of the city turned out.

"I've seen films of DeGaulle re-entering Paris after the recapture of France, and the Allies marching up Italy," said Beatle George Harrison, in Adelaide. "Without wanting to draw comparisons, the expressions on the faces today were similar to the faces of people freed from captivity."

The 1960s was a decade of change and, however it is considered, the Beatles were an important part of the soundtrack. But it seems they, too, were looking for liberation—spiritual liberation. Instead of going the traditional route, though, they took a turn that led to the spiritualism of the East.

They weren't the first, but we shouldn't underestimate the influence they had in popularising Eastern thinking to the West. Their popularity ensured others would follow, and lead to a wider acceptance of what we now term New Age thinking.

A generation and more after the Beatles, normative Christianity is under threat. In two ways:

Consumer religion

"Consumer religions" is a term researcher Adam Possamai (in a recent *Australian Religion Studies Review*) uses to describe the current situation. In a study he made of 35 New Agers, he found that people actually consume "products" in an effort to discover or enhance their personal spirituality. Many of the products came from the East, but it's now far broader.

Those searching for a "spiritual experience" can visit a healing centre for a few days, participate in a "vision quest," have an introduction to shamanism, purchase crystals or learn astrology. What was once considered demonic, he adds, is now simply for sale.

It's true! Today you can walk down the street and be accosted by a palm reader, be enticed by advertisements for astral travel or the secrets of American Indian spiritism (or buy one of their "spirit—or dream—catchers" for your home), or visit a clairvoyant at your local Sunday market.

For many, Christianity is simply another product in the spiritual market. But because Christianity is the traditional religion of the West, it lacks the glamour and exotic appeal of the New Age product.

Consumer Christianity

"Pluralism is the cause of the crisis of meaning in modernity," say Peter Berger and Thomas Luckman in *Modernity, Pluralism and the Crisis of Meaning*. They added, "The majority of people feel insecure and lost in a confusing world full of possibilities of interpretation of which some are linked to alternative ways of life."

They see this impacting the church in several ways: membership is now by a deliberate choice, not birth or geography; churches now need to consider the wishes of members; and churches must prove themselves in the "free market," because people who "buy" a particular brand of Christian faith become a group of consumers and, they emphasise, the customer is always right.

The problem with this consumer approach to Christianity is that its emphasis is on self, not Christ and the Word. Consumers are motivated by considerations such as, *What will it cost?* and, *What will I get out of it?* Brand loyalty then becomes an issue of whether it suits me rather than *Is this what God wants of me?* Christians who approach their Christianity in this way will never fully mature.

Consumer choice

It's true that in our consumer age Christianity is often considered another product, with Adventism simply a brand line. We can't change that, but we can adapt our thinking to allow for it.

In the consumer age, we first need to be certain of what it is we're selling, and why a person should buy it. Next, our product needs to be based on certainties that go way beyond the mere feel-good. Finally, we need to know how to best sell our product.

Within the church the wishes of the "customers" should be considered, but its direction and teachings must remain based on something more substantial than mere common consent: it must be founded on God and His Word.

So, what is the answer? No, *who* is the answer? Any response to the consumer society must be based in the person of Jesus. It's crass to call salvation a product, but that's what we're selling. And salvation is only ever found in Him, and that will never change.

Only in Him are we truly liberated. Understanding that is the first step toward tackling our consumer age.

LIVING IN THE LAND
OF THE BLAND

Melbourne's Catholic archbishop, George Pell, recently said, "The great temptation for religion in our society is to just merge into the general cultural background. The bland leading the bland" (*The Bulletin*, April 27, 1999).

Bland? That's the danger in a cosmopolitan, multicultural society where most beliefs and philosophies are tolerated. It's the danger when policies are developed by opinion polls and attitudes by the media. Unless there's a deliberate attempt to remain distinctive, it's like collecting pots of colours and mixing them together, they become a sludgy grey-brown—bland.

The Christian is called to stand out, to give flavour to the world, to bring light, not to follow the beat of the bland. Archbishop Pell's comment is a challenge to all Christians, including Seventh-day Adventists who may be tempted to follow the Laodicean brand of bland. It's a call to maintain our Christian–Adventist distinctiveness.

Faith focused

That means remaining faith focused, for our ultimate hope is in Jesus Christ. Faith is more than a mental assent to Jesus' life, death, resurrection and promised return. It's living a life of trust in Him, making His promises our hope and joy. That's life changing, life invigorating.

And in Him there is security—the kind no other philosophy or religion offers. He's with us in the dark moments, in our times of despair and sorrow. When we feel He may not be there, He is. In the times of success, the moments of satisfaction, and when joy fills us and we don't even bother to think of Him, He's there.

Faith says that in the face of death itself, God is there and He is on our side (see Romans 8:37-39). Knowing that can lead to a vibrant life.

To be like Jesus

Out of faith in Jesus comes a life for Jesus—living like Jesus. That means taking time apart to pray and meditate, as He did. It means empathy and concern for those who are less fortunate, and offering practical help to them, as He did.

It means loving our enemies, as He did. That would certainly stand out in the land of the bland.

To be like Jesus means being willing to take risks for God, as He did. To speak for Him as opportunities present. And to watch more carefully for those opportunities, encourage those opportunities, treasure them and be prepared for them.

Most real changes in people's lives are made one-on-one, not in programs and events. Church programs and events can help with information, but reflecting Jesus is something that can only be done by individuals who are committed to Him.

Jesus gave time to the individual: to Nicodemus, to the paralytic at the pool, to the woman at the well. He took the time to help them with their real needs—there was nothing superficial about Him, nothing bland.

Advent focused

It's easier to sing "This world is not my home, I'm just a-passing thru . . ." than to live it, particularly if we are financially secure. We often limit our picture of heaven to living in five-star luxury, something that's attainable here. And those of us who've not ascended to such delights can be blinded by thinking that this should be our goal—particularly when society equates wealth with success.

Realising there is something better coming—and coming soon—helps us see our lives in proper perspective. That doesn't mean we don't strive to achieve (the parable of the talents teaches that we should), but we strive with an eye to the kingdom.

Consider Abraham: He was establishing a nation for God and he had most things a person could want, but he looked forward to the city of God being established (Hebrews 11:10).

Being true

Moving away from the bland means being true to our distinctive beliefs. The Sabbath, for instance. No room here for blurring its edges; no downplaying it for the sake of convenience, and no compromise.

Lifestyle, for instance. Believing that God created us as a whole, balanced package consisting of our mental, physical, social and spiritual sides, means attempting to live a healthy, well-balanced life. Taking time for God; time for re-creation; time for socialising, particularly with family; time for mind stretching.

Being true means our convictions have significance in our life. We may live in the land of the bland, but we're called to something better, to stand like the brave with our faith to the fore.

CHRIST AT CHRISTMAS?
YES, PLEASE!

Sometimes a picture says it best. The December 1998 cover of *Signs of the Times* (USA) is one of those occasions. It has a picture of the manger scene with the wise men bringing gifts. Serious men bearing serious gifts.

Stunned men bearing serious gifts.

In the foreground is someone from the 20th century, a bit of a jokester with a jokester's gift—a baby-sized Santa suit.

Hey, who needs a saviour if you can have a Santa? And two millennia after the birth, why should children get excited about a Christmas creche with a baby doll in a feed trough surrounded by adult dolls, when up the way is a man in a red suit who's promising them whatever they want?

Some say the problem with Christmas is its origins are in a pagan festival. But the past isn't the problem with Christmas; it's the present. During the season to be merry, we're confronted with the profane and the divine competing with each other for our attention; the challenge of materialism against the spiritual. Who's winning?

The story of the birth of Jesus rates less media time than the story of Santa. And the Santa story has come a long way from its origins of a pious Christian bishop known for his concern and care for children. While Charles Dickens's *A Christmas Carol* is probably responsible for popularising the day, Coca-Cola is responsible for giving us an obese, jolly, red-robed (Coca-Cola red) Santa. Now it's a competition: The man who brings gifts against the Man who is the gift.

Wait a minute. If Jesus and Santa are both a part of Christmas, what happens when a child discovers Santa was their dad? Where does that place Jesus? As just another Christmas legend? Up there with Rudolph the red-nosed reindeer and Frosty the snowman?

That's the danger.

That's why we who follow Christ have a responsibility to refocus Christmas. We can't let the fat man in the red suit win this battle. He has nothing to offer compared to the Child in the manger.

Another question: What kind of Christ will we emphasise at Christmas?

We'd think it sacrilegious to put Jesus in a Santa suit. But in our imaginations we attempt to suit Him out to fit our preconceptions. We want a comfortable Jesus. Not the One who asks for commitment. Not the One who says, "Take up your cross and follow Me." Not the One who says, "Whoever lays down their life for My sake shall gain it."

We take the comfortable Christ when we suit Him out in the Santa outfit as exalted gift-giver, put Him in the clothes of the rich uncle to whom we go with our requests, in the outfit of the favoured aunt who never yells at us.

Or worse, we leave Him in the manger. That means He can't challenge us with His life. He can't reach us with His death. He can't confront us with the gospel.

The babe in the manger is manageable—cute. A cute and cuddly Christ can be kept at arm's length. That's nothing like the New Testament Christ who confronts us with in-your-face reality—read the Sermon on the Mount; see Him set an example of helping the helpless; hear Him tell us we must be born again.

But it's a reality that's good news. Listen: "I, if I be lifted up, will draw all to me"; "Whoever believes will have eternal life"; "I will come back for you."

The angels heralded the birth; now it's up to us to herald the life, the death, the resurrection and the promise of the return. Especially at Christmas.

IN PRAISE
OF CITY LIVING

You don't have to tell me of the advantages of country living. I grew up in the country. There's country-boy blood flowing through my veins. Given a choice, that's where I'd live.

But what would happen if all Adventists left the cities? Imagine closing down all churches and schools in the cities, and, maybe, setting up country enclaves to become a people of commuters, or establishing industries in the country. I guess we could leave our institutions, particularly our hospitals, in the cities, but again we'd have to commute.

Keep your imagination working. How could we do serious evangelism in your capital city without an Adventist presence?

Public evangelism? Sure, we could set up evangelism teams (satellite evangelism could be useful) to venture into the cities to run programs, win a few people, and then help them leave the cities (so they could attend an Adventist church).

If we're serious about the task of Christianity, taking the gospel to the world, we can't ignore the cities—that's where most people are. That means Adventists living in cities, for we can't be "light" and "salt" from afar. Besides, people in cities are more open to change than those in the country, and they need to see the Adventist option in action.

So many Adventists can't contemplate a choice outside the city—they wouldn't be able to support themselves or their family anywhere else. That's true in Australia and New Zealand as well as the developing world. And we desperately need Adventist Christian influence in the supercities of the developing world.

Cities are not evil in themselves. What goes on in cities can be evil (and this country boy knows that what goes on in the country can be evil also). Abraham searched for a city whose builder was God. At the end of the millennium, it's the city of God that comes to earth, and it's a high-rise city (Revelation 21:2, 16).

About now someone will be feeling uncomfortable and want to remind me of Ellen White's comments about the advantages of country living. (See, for instance, the compilation *Country Living*, which is available at Adventist Book Centres.)

Gottfried Oosterwal makes an important point: "As in Scripture, she [Ellen White] warns us of the dangers of the city, calling believers away from these places of evil. But when she speaks of the city in the light of God's compassion, she urges the believers to pray for the prosperity of the city and to live and work there for its redemption" (in Richard Lehmann, Jack Mahon and Borge Schantz, eds, *Cast the Net on the Right Side*).

He's right. It's an education to take out the index to Ellen White's writings and scan the entries under "city." The warnings are there about the dangers of city living—particularly for families—but then you find her encouraging the building of churches, schools and institutions in the cities. She asks the question, "Why should not families who know the present truth settle in these cities and villages, to set up there the standard of Christ . . . ?" (*Christian Service*, page 180).

Importantly, she says first-century Christians living in the city of Antioch are an example to ministers and members who live in the "great cities of the world today." She calls for "living representatives of Bible truth" to live in these great cities (*The Acts of the Apostles*, page 158).

And isn't being part of a community the best form of evangelism? It's certainly the most successful. Even the greatest of our evangelists and the best hi-tech programs are mostly dependent for their success on Adventists encouraging friends to attend.

For some, country living is their lot. Good for them! For others, it will come only when they retire to their cabin next to the sea of glass. In the meantime, let's encourage, pray for and support city Adventists as they attempt to be living representatives of God's truth.

And let's praise them for their courage as they let their light shine in a dark place.

HERE'S TO
RESPONSIBLE DRINKING

Alcohol means fun. That's the image the alcohol industry gives its product through the media. It's accepted. It's sold as a part of any celebration (particularly by winners of sporting events). It's the answer to that "hard-earned thirst."

The call is for responsible drinking rather than abstaining. But Adventists have always been on the wagon, saying no to alcohol. Should we change?

1. Out of touch?

Even some Adventists feel an anti-alcohol stance is something that is somehow unique, out-of-touch and without support from others. Wrong. You can't be a good Mormon and drink alcohol. And you would be thrown out of the Salvation Army.

2. Show me a text

No, you find a Bible text that says, "Thou shalt not drink alcohol." But even the casual reader soon discovers that we're to put the best possible in our bodies. That we're temples of the Holy Spirit (1 Corinthians 6:18, 19)—the context is about sexual immorality, but the principle is still there. Of course, there is the instruction, "Let us purify ourselves from everything that contaminates body and spirit . . . ," which covers whatever we eat or drink (2 Corinthians 7:1). And what about 1 Corinthians 10:31?

3. The Adventist approach

There are solid Bible principles for good living. These are Christian principles that can't be tagged to a particular denomination. The anti-alcohol stance of the Adventist Church comes from our holistic approach to Christian living. We have a concern for the physical, mental and social as well as the spiritual, noting that each impacts on the other. This is one of the most attractive elements of the Adventist Church.

4. The embarrassment

On a broader front, alcohol among Christians is a major embarrassment in the Middle East and in Muslim countries (about 25 per cent of the world's population). Christians are best known among Muslims for two negatives: alcohol and pornography. Both are banned in Muslim countries; both are freely available in Christian countries. Their use of alcohol is a strong argument against Christianity in these countries. We may not be able to do much for the overall impression given by Christian countries, but as individuals we need to do better.

5. Insert your lecture here

Insert here your lecture to yourself about the harmful personal effects of drinking even the smallest amount of alcohol. Only the wine industry is actually convinced that wine is good for you. (It actually may help your heart, but it is drilling holes in your liver at the same time.) And, of course, any impairment of your decision-making abilities may lead to harm to someone else.

6. Street drugs are OK?

Any who drink alcohol are actually saying OK to recreational drug taking because that's what they're doing. And any stand they may have against street drugs is limited because street drug use is another form of recreational drug use. Sure, one is legal and the other isn't, but making a drug legal doesn't make it any less damaging, only less likely to be tainted.

7. The killer drug

Those who drink alcohol are saying OK to the drug that's the biggest killer of young people in Australia. They're saying OK to the drug that causes more deaths by drowning than any other influence. They're saying OK to the drug that causes an incredible number of deaths on the roads.

8. Changing perceptions

The public perception of alcohol is slowly changing, and becoming more negative. Organisers of public family functions now openly advertise that their event will be alcohol-free. On New Year's Eve in Melbourne this year,* public "trouble spots" were declared alcohol-free. Public reaction will probably see the banning of alcohol advertising within 10 years. Will we lead the charge?

9. Example

Everybody is a hero to someone. That means our example is important. How tragic if my example leads another to struggle with alcohol (one in 10 are predisposed to alcoholism, and even they don't know it until they try it). How would you feel if it were a close friend? Your child? Your grandchild? And what of our Christian witness? We need to be heroes for Christ.

With alcohol, responsible drinking begins with saying, "No, thank you."

*1998.

SHOULD CHURCHES
BE ACCOUNTABLE?

If the church were a business, it would be simple to measure success: you'd find it there in the bottom line. Because a business has a mission that focuses on profitability, success includes such relatively easily measured variables as profit margins, market share and sales.

But how do you measure success in a nonprofit organisation (and there are at least 92,000 in Australia, ranging from churches to charitable trusts to the local darts club)? What measure should be used to test if a church is successful or not? The number of people in the pews each Sabbath? Baptisms? Percentage growth? Tithe paid? Goal setting is certainly an excellent way of measuring achievement, but is that success?

Churches (like all nonprofit organisations) are notorious for their inefficient use of human resources. Not that this is a bad thing. A scientist who visits shut-ins, or a carpenter who helps plan worship programs may not use their primary skills (which would give peak efficiency), but they give and gain something quite different from their involvement. This "something" can't be measured.

Besides, who wants a church pastor who, while efficiently visiting church members and allowing precisely 30 minutes per visit, can't spend an afternoon helping a grieving family cope with a sudden loss, or drop everything to share the message with an inquirer?

Diana Leat* suggests that rather than attempting to measure *success*, nonprofit organisations would do better to seek *accountability*. She calls for accountability in four areas:

1. Fiscal accountability

Obvious? But this is more than making sure the church isn't in the red or that the ledger balances. How was/is the money used? Does it help to achieve the goals and mission of the church?

A church with money in the bank needs to ask, why? A church without money in the bank needs to ask, why? Fiscal accountability calls for proper accounting procedures and the proper use of money.

2. Process accountability

Are the proper processes, the proper procedures, being followed? This means first taking time to work through what the procedures are. Many procedures are natural and need little thought. Others, such as the church's responsibility for accommodation in the event of an emergency (as exists in some states), demand a written manual of procedures.

The importance of proper procedures is simply illustrated: What procedure is in place if a church member doesn't attend your church for two consecutive weeks? Would the person be missed? Is there a procedure? If not, what procedure could be put in place that would plug that hole? Who would be responsible?

3. Quality accountability

This is about the quality of the programs and services the church has for its members and for the community. It seems easy to be concerned about the quality of workmanship in a church building extension, but why not for the Sabbath school or the church's outreach programs?

What would happen to Sabbath school classes if the church insisted that teachers undergo training before being allowed to teach? That they attend a refresher course every six months? That they be at Sabbath school an hour before class time for prayer and sharing? And that those not willing or unable to commit themselves to this process were dropped from the teaching roster? (Would we see larger—but better—classes?)

Every department and program could come under similar quality controls. Spiritual gifts are never harmed by training or accountability.

4. Priority accountability

This is perhaps the most important, because it impacts on the others. A good emphasis among churches over the past few years has seen the development of mission statements, where the church's core mission is spelled out.

Having (through a mission statement or some other method) discovered what the priorities of a church are, accountability demands that church activities and programs be regularly assessed to see if they help fulfil the church's mission ("the relevance or appropriateness of its work," says Ms Leat).

The call for accountability is not a call to develop administration overload within the local church (that's a poor priority). But it is recognition that a church that is serious about accountability will be a church of excellence.

*Diana Leat, "Voluntary Organisations and Accountability: Theory and Practice" in *The Third Sector: Comparative Studies in Nonprofit Organisations*, Walter de Gruyter, Berlin, 1990.

SHOULD WE FEAR CHANGE?

I've heard the calls for change.

Some seem to weep like the old priests and Levites in Ezra's time who, when they saw the foundation of the new temple, realised a former glory had passed (Ezra 3:12). Maybe there was a former glory in the Adventist Church, but a former glory is always just that, "former."

Some call for change as if they want to keep up with the latest trends, in the name of relevancy. But fad-chasing simply leads to confusion and instability.

Neither position should be dismissed out of hand. We have much to learn from the past, and a church in the end-time must he relevant to the end-time.

There must be a place for a valid call for change, a call that reaches all levels of the church.

Those who are administrators of the church must study and implement efficiencies so that we can be more effective in our mission. That means change.

For many years there have been calls for the church to have less duplication. Are some of the levels of the division, the unions and the conferences necessary? Should we rationalise some of the roles performed at each level? Should some conferences amalgamate? Again we're talking change.

Local churches are currently going through a minor revolution. There is no longer a sameness in our churches as each develops its own personalities. One pastor I know is currently reviving a dying church by developing a very conservative worship program. Members unhappy with churches experimenting in more innovative worship styles now attend his church. Change and counterchange.

Talking about change at the local level is difficult. We all see so clearly the need for change at other levels and sometimes wonder when "they" are going to do something about it. At church level we're the ones responsible—and what you want to change may not be what I would change. How do we resolve that conflict?

Perhaps it's time to look for change in the most basic building block of the church, you and me. Here are a few things we could work on:

- Adventists are reading their Bibles less than they were a generation ago. To call ourselves the "people of the Book," as some did just a couple of decades ago, would now be a joke. Is it because we think we have all the answers and don't need Bible study anymore? Or maybe we're just satisfied with the milk of the Word when we need to chew on the gluten of the Word. Finding 30 minutes each day for God's Word wouldn't cause much of a radical change to anyone's lifestyle. Yet, it could cause a radical change in their life.
- We don't talk much about prayer in the Adventist Church. That should change. What would happen in your church if every time there was conflict, or a serious decision to be made, the congregation spent longer on its knees than in discussion?
- Can we become more open to the Spirit's leading? We have guidance through the Bible and the writings of Ellen White. Let's not belittle either, but with so much instruction, it's tempting to try to interpret it to fit any particular need so that we don't have to be open to the Spirit's leading. How long has it been since you were involved in a serious time of study and prayer as a part of your searching, or your church's searching, for the Holy Spirit's guidance through a particular problem or decision? Could this bring change to your life? To your church?
- Can you imagine your church if each member determined to follow what Christ called His "new" command: "Love one another. As I have loved you, so you must love one another" (John 13:34)?

Love? Like Jesus? His love is constant. "I the Lord do not change," says God (Malachi 3:6). He begins that little book with, "I love you." Thank God, that never changes.

Dare we attempt to change, to be more like Him?

No-one would deny we need to become more Christlike, to be more open to the Spirit, to pray more, or to study our Bibles more. But imagine how this would change your church. Or how it would impact on your community.

Maybe, just maybe, it would also help us to make better decisions on those other areas of change that are necessary at various levels in our church.

Should we be serious about change? Of course. We have nothing to fear from change unless we move outside the Lord's will.

The most frightening thought of all is this: If we don't change, we'll remain the same.

God forbid!

DOLLAR-DRIVEN
CHURCH?

"I can't understand why, when we discuss the business of the church, we spend so much time discussing money," said my new-found friend, referring to the meetings we were attending.

The meetings were out-of-town and meant staying for a few nights in a hostel. My room-mate was a layperson, a Pacific islander. Naturally, we spent a good deal of time discussing the church. I was particularly interested in discovering what was happening with the church in his area.

But his comment struck home.

If money, as it seems, does make the world go round, will it take money for the Adventist Church to have an impact on the world?

It takes money to run public evangelistic campaigns. To have an extensive education program. To publish books and magazines. To record videos and television programs. To build and maintain churches. To place missionaries. To help the needy. To run hospitals. To succeed in the health food work.

In many ways, the church *is* a business. And much of the church needs to run on good business lines for it to be financially viable. But the church must be much more than a mere business run by dark-suited accountants whose only concern is to maintain profitability.

The main business of the Adventist Church is not in keeping books balanced, but in helping to establish the kingdom of God. We have a Christ to share, a mission to proclaim, and a fellowship to build.

When we lose that focus we lose our sense of mission, and we lose the vision. Worse, we lose our reason for being.

I've seen treasurers, from General Conference level through to the local church level, struggle to find funds for outreach projects when so much of the budget has been taken up in maintaining the structure we already have.

After the comment by my Adventist brother, from what is a developing country, I'm beginning to wonder if they don't have an advantage by having virtually no budget to worry about.

In those areas the church must, of necessity, be run on faith. Is that one of the secrets to the greater success of evangelism in developing countries?

Most of us live in cities and towns, where, if the skylines were ever dominated by churches, they're now dominated by banks, insurance companies and businesses; organisations that place money first. That has had its impact on the church.

Too often I've heard it said (and, to be honest, have thought it myself) that if only we had a few more dollars we would see more success. Or we could have a greater impact in the community. And, in a sense, it's true.

But the church will not fulfil its mission by finding a few more dollars. For it is "'not by might nor by power [or money], but by my Spirit,' says the Lord Almighty" (Zechariah 4:6). That's where the real strength of the church is.

The completion of the work of God is not dependent on money. Tertullian, a Christian in the second century, said, "Nothing that is God's is attainable by money." A dollar-driven church can only fail.

Don't get me wrong. I'm not saying that we should stop paying our tithes and offerings. Far from it. We should be more careful and more faithful with what we return to the Lord and His church than at any other time.

In fact, how generous we are toward the Lord's cause is a good indicator of where our personal focus is.

Treasurers and boards at local churches have to decide how they will budget to maintain their church and outreach programs. That will never change. And it's often a struggle to meet the demands. That struggle happens at all levels of the church. But the comment my friend made should make us pause and think. We should not even make it *appear* that money is our main interest. For it isn't.

Even those parts of the church that are businesses, such as our medical, publishing and health food work, need to understand their main function is not a financial one. That merely belittles their role.

Let's not make the mistake another church made by focusing on its wealth only to discover that in reality it was wretched, pitiful, *poor*, blind and naked.

SALT, NOT MUSTARD

SALT, NOT MUSTARD

I'm angry. And I'm struggling to keep it to the kind of anger that would turn over money tables in the temple (righteous indignation) and not have it mixed with anger of another kind.

I'm angry because I write this just after full-page advertisements have appeared in newspapers in New Zealand and Papua New Guinea that are strongly anti-Catholic in nature, but with "Seventh-day Adventist" connections. The church has rightly attempted to distance itself from these advertisements, but the damage is incredible—in some cases, irredeemable.

I'm sure those behind the advertisements are well intentioned. The tragedy is that they have demonstrated a lack of Christian maturity that denies plain biblical counsel and that of Ellen White, and they have shown little understanding of social history.

Letter to the editor

In 1896, one of my predecessors as the Australia–New Zealand *Signs of the Times* editor, W A Colcord, received a letter from Ellen White. It took him to task: "I feel hurt when I see that so many decided thrusts are made against the Catholics. Preach the truth, but restrain the words which show a harsh spirit; for such words cannot help or enlighten anyone" (*Counsels to Writers and Editors*, pages 64-5).

Her concern was that displays of anti-Catholic sentiment would not allow the truth to have its impact: "Many Catholics read the *Echo* [*Signs of the Times* was then known as the *Bible Echo and Signs of the Times*] and among the number are honest souls who will accept the truth. But there is such a thing as shutting the door in their faces as they are about to enter."

Salt or mustard?

Jesus called His followers to be salt, to enhance life through their witness and teaching. He did not call us to be mustard. Mustard delivers an explosion of flavour that, for some, affronts the taste.

Does being "salt" mean we deny truth as we understand it? Of course it doesn't. But we need to be wise about its presentation.

We've chosen to be Seventh-day Adventists, which means we're committed to certain teachings, life practices and a philosophy that differs from other denominations. But do we want to be known as a people who oppose those who don't believe as we do? Presbyterians because they worship on Sunday? Uniting Church people because they don't baptise by immersion? Baptists because they believe in the secret rapture teaching?

Do we want to be known as a people with an anti-Catholic, anti-Presbyterian, anti-Uniting, anti-Baptist message? Rather, shouldn't we be known by what we stand *for* and that we have a pro-Christ message? Life enhancers will want to promote the One who is life.

For several generations, Adventist evangelists have known they needed to begin their series with what we stand for: Jesus; the Bible (the basis of the archaeology approach); Creation; the Resurrection; health; and so on. These same evangelists understand that when they come to sharing our historicist approach to prophecy and the differences we have with other denominations and belief systems they need to follow Paul's counsel—to speak the truth in love.

But weren't we anti-Catholic?

There was a time when we, along with other Protestant denominations, were strongly anti-Catholic. Early last century (1909-15), W W Prestcott edited *Protestant Magazine*, a quarterly in the United States "protesting against ecclesiastical error and promoting gospel truth." During its brief life, it enjoyed broad support among Adventists and the broader Protestant communities, creating some lively correspondence from Catholics.

Even 50 years ago, Catholic baiting was popular among Protestants in Australia and New Zealand. Thankfully, we now live in a more accepting society, one that is rightly outraged when one group tries to put another down.

Some will be tempted to think this all sounds a little too "politically correct," but we need to consider the example Jesus set.

Jesus treated harshly those who had truth, but abused it (see, for instance, Matthew 23). He was accepting and gentle with truth seekers. We who know not the heart must assume we are constantly dealing with such truth seekers. Our past is no defence for adopting damaging, confrontational tactics today.

I'm angry because these recent advertisements effectively shut the door (to use Ellen White's term) for many who may have been willing to listen to who we are and what we have to offer. My church and Christ is misrepresented by this kind of action.

We're called to be salt, not mustard.

SIN AND SINNERS

The almost appointment of a practising gay (homosexual) bishop in 2003, and the reality in the United States placed homosexuality in the church on the agenda. In Australia in the same year a vote by the Uniting Church's National Assembly allowed individual presbyteries to accept people for ordination, candidature for ministry or placement in ministry on a case-by-case basis.

"This recommendation is seen by many as opening the door to the acceptance of a homosexual person for ordination or placement in ministry," said the president of the Uniting Church, the Reverend Dr Dean Drayton.*

The high-profile Reverend Fred Nile certainly saw it as opening the door for the "ordination of practising homosexuals" and resigned from the church.

The superintendent of Wesley Mission Sydney, the Reverend Dr Gordon Moyes, called it a symptom of the malaise in "our church." "The Christian church does not have to be popular in society to survive, but it must be faithful to Jesus Christ," he says.

The result is "terminal" with little support "in the pews," he adds. Some 24,000 members from more than 500 Uniting Church congregations have signed a petition protesting the decision. And there's little support outside the church if a ninemsn web poll was correct. The question "Do you support the ordination of homosexuals as church ministers?" received a 26 per cent (16,183) yes response and a 74 per cent (45,088) no response.

The Bible and homosexuality

While there have been attempts to interpret differently Bible statements against acts of homosexuality (as found, for instance, in Leviticus 18:22; 20:13; Romans 1:26-32; and 1 Corinthians 6:9), the plain meaning and intent is clear. Practising homosexuality is sin—as are a list of other sexual practices. In fact it is difficult to defend from the Bible anything but sexual intimacy between a man and a woman within marriage.

Sin? Some feel sensitive about calling any conduct sin, particularly homosexuality, because political correctness suggests it an improper response. And, before we who do not fall under the spell of this particular sin begin to feel too self-righteous, we must all recognise that we too are guilty of sins that need tackling. All are in need of God's grace and forgiveness.

Homosexuals need understanding as much as adulterers, thieves, gossips and liars. Not permission, understanding. Hate or disgust is a response that is also sinful.

A recent survey of almost 20,000 Australians (published in the *Australia New Zealand Journal of Public Health*, April 2003) found that 1.6 per cent of men identified themselves as homosexual and 0.9 per cent as bisexual. For women, 0.8 per cent identified themselves as homosexual and 1.4 per cent as bisexual. A higher percentage reported "same-sex attraction and homosexual experience," which can be interpreted in various ways.

Knowing that only a small percentage are homosexual does not belittle the problem. It helps us understand that, in any group of 100 Adventists, there are probably two who have homosexual tendencies. This is not a call for a witch hunt, but for understanding. If you choose the witch-hunt path, don't forget to include other sins as well—including the ever-popular pride (the "most hopeless, the most incurable" sin, *Christ's Object Lessons*, page 154) and backbiting.

There's continuing debate about whether homosexuality is learned behaviour or a predisposition a person is born with. But neither position takes away choice of actions any more than others—kleptomaniacs or alcoholics, for instance—have choices in theirs. As difficult as these choices may be.

Sin and sinners

The Uniting Church's National Assembly may revisit its decision; that's for them to sort out. Our responsibility is within our own church. And our response must be biblical.

So, how do we treat homosexuals? No, that's too limiting. How do we treat sinners? Jesus is the example. He loves sinners. He welcomes sinners. He forgives sinners. You see this in His ministry.

When we confront sin, whatever its label, we do well to remember His righteousness and our sinfulness. We do well to remember that we're all on a pilgrimage that's more successful as we help lift each other to a higher level. We do well to remember that we deny our Lord if we confront sin with anything but patience and love.

If we follow the biblical model, those with homosexual tendencies should be as welcome and involved in church as any with sinful tendencies—that's all of us. It's the practising of sins that creates problems that need addressing.

*Most information comes from a July 31, 2003, *New Life* report.

THE HUMAN TOUCH

She was blind. I touched her on the shoulder and spoke to let her know I had to get by to my seat. The plane wasn't full so there was an empty seat between us.

I made a couple of comments, but they seemed to be ignored, so I settled in for the flight home. Once in the air she opened a laptop computer and worked away at it.

The stewards were impressive in how attentive they were to her needs. (Congratulations, Virgin Blue.)

About 20 minutes from landing, she dropped something onto the floor. I picked it up for her. That started the conversation.

She was an executive member of a blind society and was on her way to meetings in Melbourne. They were hoping to make decisions at the meetings that would help a variety of groups working for people with disabilities to coordinate their efforts better.

Well travelled, she'd spent 12 months living in the United States and was planning to do more trips overseas. She obviously didn't plan to let blindness slow her down.

I asked her what dumb questions sighted people asked her. (I didn't want to ask one of those dumb questions.) I was surprised when she told of those who asked her about other disabilities she must have. She was obviously annoyed by those who assume that because she has one disability she must have a whole raft of them. Worse was when she was treated as if she were dumb as well as blind.

She asked what I did.

I find it an interesting study of human nature when I'm asked that question. I can't wait to get to the "Seventh-day Adventist Church" part to see what reaction there is. The reaction varies from a vague kind of look as if they have never heard of Adventists, to, "My auntie is one of those."

Sometimes it becomes a conversation stopper or dampener.

When I told her what I did and that I worked for the Seventh-day Adventist Church, her reaction was immediate: "I know Seventh-day Adventists!"

"How do you know them?"

"I once went to a blind camp they held."

She couldn't remember where it was, but it sounded like it had been held at Crosslands in Sydney and, from her age, it would have been some time ago. She said that, for her, the camp had been a little too controlled, but conceded she was much older than most of the others attending and understood why it was that way.

She seemed impressed by what the church was doing for blind children. The conversation then drifted in another area.

I was flying home after attending the South Pacific Division's midyear meetings with an emphasis on evangelism and effective "branding" of the Adventist Church. In other words, following the Lord's commission, and projecting a positive message to the community. Effective branding also involves the consistent use of the church name and logo.

This woman had a positive impression of the church through a program she'd participated in. She hadn't been to an evangelistic campaign—at least not one she mentioned. The church logo and how the print appeared under the logo (something logophiles worry about) had no impact because she couldn't see it.

It was the program, one that met her specific needs, and the human contact made at that time that made the impression. She was a reminder that it's the people of the Adventist Church who can have a far greater impact than any other resource the church—and God—has.

We can spend millions advertising the church, attempting to sell it with McDonald's and Ford cars on television, to create an image. We can have the most consistent branding possible. We can run the most successful evangelistic program of all time. But all these will ultimately fail without the added warmth and friendship of Adventist people.

That sound you can hear is applause (mine) for evangelism and effective branding. But we, the people of the church, can supply something those things can't—a listening ear, a friendly smile and an attitude that says that being an Adventist is an attractive proposition.

We waited while the others left the plane. We were last because she needed help off and the stewards had asked her to wait. I was in no hurry, so we chatted some more. I don't know if my conversation helped add to the positive impression she had of the Adventist Church. I hope it did.

IF YOU WERE A GUEST
TO YOUR CHURCH . . .

If you were a first-time guest to your church, would you bother to return?

Is it possible to put our own church under that same magnifying glass we put on the churches we visit? Or to gain some insight into how guests feel when they first come to our church? Particularly if the guest were a non-Christian or a non-Adventist? It's worth a try.

First impressions: the plant

As a first-time guest, what are your first impressions as you drive into the car park, or walk onto the church property? Do the shrubs and plants look like someone cares? What about the paintwork? Spider webs anywhere?

What about church signage? Does it look like it needs a coat of paint? Should the phone number have been updated two pastors ago?

Yes, I know the church is "people," and we should have greater concerns for the people than the building we worship in, but the place we worship in also communicates a message. We would be embarrassed if the preacher weren't appropriately dressed for the occasion. We should also be embarrassed if the church and its grounds weren't likewise appropriately "clothed."

We need to take care that where we worship is representative, even if we don't have a church building. I remember a church group that met in the Independent Order of Oddfellows hall in their town. I have no idea why the decision was made to worship there—it may have been quite valid (and I mention it because they now have one of the best church buildings in the town)—but at the time, though, to have an Adventist church meeting in the Oddfellows hall must have sent a negative message.

As a guest to your church, how would you view the decor as you walked into the foyer, then into the church itself? Friendly? Inviting? Contemporary? Or something else?

First impressions: the people

As a guest to your church, how are you greeted? (Are you greeted?) Is it appropriate? Do you feel welcome? Do you have to ask where the children's Sabbath school divisions are? Are you given a church bulletin? A hymnal, if necessary? Would you be helped to a Sabbath school class or seat? Would those who sit next to you acknowledge your presence? Or would you be ignored? Would there be sensitivity to your desires if you wanted to be ignored?

Next impressions . . .

As a first-time guest, would you know what you were supposed to do when Sabbath school classes begin? Would you understand what they were talking about in the Sabbath school class? Would you be involved in an appropriate way? Would there be a theological dogfight? Would you feel uncomfortable?

During church, would it feel like you needed instructions to follow what was happening? When to stand? When to sit? When to kneel? Would there be a sense of joy in worship and praise? A sense of wonder as people are brought closer to the throne of God? Does your church speak in Adventese that a first-time guest would either have to guess at or have translated?

Lasting impressions . . .

As a first-time guest, what would be your lasting impressions? Would you go away thinking it an experience you endured, something to laugh about with your friends? Would you think you'd been caught in a time warp for two hours? Or would you go away wishing you could have stayed longer, wanting to come back?

But most importantly, do you think you would leave having met Jesus? In the teaching and preaching? In the people you met? Would you leave knowing Jesus cares about you?

Just a game?

Is this just a game? No. This is much more. This is about how healthy your church is. And one of the best signs of a healthy church is one where a first-time guest can come, feel welcomed and want to come back again. A healthy church is one where church members continually bring guests to church because they're so excited about what is happening there. (Anyone reading this from a church like that probably turned the page several paragraphs ago, wondering why anyone would write on something so obvious.)

If you were a first-time guest to your church, would you bother to return? If not, why not? What can you do about it? No, *What will you do about it?* For a first-time guest at your church the preaching begins with the first impression—and that's even before they enter the building.

LESSONS FROM AN OLYMPIC EXPERIENCE

After the Olympics,* I have to admit, there were many moments when I felt proud to be an Australian. (Those from other countries who wish to avoid excessive amounts of Aussie self-congratulation may want to move directly to "Evan from Promotions.")

The opening ceremony didn't have the "cringe" factor we feared. In fact, it was quite moving.

More Australian gold was won at this Olympics than any other (yes, yes, there were more events at these Olympics). But even those who missed out did us proud: remember the distraught Jane Saville, the 20-kilometre walker disqualified only 120 metres from the winner's tape? Once she'd recovered from the shock, she graciously accepted the judges' decision. She may have lost the race, but she won on attitude.

The 400-metre final with Cathy Freeman was among the most-watched events of the games. Nineteen million misty-eyed Australians watched her work through a gamut of emotions as the realisation of her victory dawned upon her. Then there was that gold-medal goal in the last second of the women's water polo.

Juan Antonio Samarach said these were the best games ever. But he has said that during the closing ceremony at every Olympic Games since he became president (with the notable exception of Atlanta).

Evan from Promotions

But what made me really proud to be an Aussie during the Olympics wasn't what happened in the pool or on the track. It was what happened in the streets of Sydney. ABC Radio formulated a politeness test to discover how friendly Sydneysiders really were during the games.

"We tried to get the best undercover man for the job," said announcer Dave Mark, "but we ended up with Evan from Promotions." Evan was dressed as a tourist, complete with an Akubra hat and a backpack with an American flag sticking out of it.

Evan's job was to look lost. He was taken to several sites in the city where he would pull out a map and appear to be working out where he was. The test was to discover how long it would take for someone to offer him help. He was to say nothing until he was approached. When he did speak, it was with an American accent (which he did rather poorly).

"I'm trying to make my way here to Circular Kway," he'd say.

After informing him that it was actually called Circular Quay, the locals would give directions.

There were times when it took a couple of minutes for help to arrive. But there were also times when they didn't have time to start the clock. The average was one minute and six seconds.

This was a gold-medal performance. Sydney passed the politeness test—a bigger test than whether the city could supply the venues and conduct the games. This was a test about how guests to our country are treated.

Meanwhile, back at the church

I wonder what would happen if Evan turned up at my church. The same principle applies. The venue may be exceptional. The music may be heavenly. The preaching may be soul stirring. But if guests feel unwanted or unwelcome, we've failed them—and our Lord.

Do we need reminding that the church is involved in the greatest competition in the universe—the great controversy? Every Sabbath we represent God's kingdom to those with whom we worship. Aiming for anything less than a PB (that's personal best) could see us off the team.

Sure, volunteers at the doors welcome guests, answer questions and give directions. That's important. But that's to be expected. And, like the volunteers at the Olympics, that's their job; that's what they're there to do.

The real test comes as you and I—average pew sitters—relate to guests. And this is something we can practise among ourselves. It isn't hard: a smile of recognition. A greeting. The sliding along the seat to share a Bible or hymnbook.

We're called to be people-friendly—just like Jesus.

Just as we would for first-time guests in our home, we should anticipate the needs of those visiting our church. We want them to appreciate the venue, enjoy the music and be inspired by the preaching. But that comes to naught if they leave feeling our church was "cold."

A one-minute-and-six-second delay in offering assistance may be a gold-medal performance for a city. The church must do better. After all, we aren't playing games.

*Sydney, 2000.

… SALT, NOT MUSTARD

THE CAROLINE DAVIS
I NEVER KNEW

Caroline Davis used to write to me, often. I rarely responded, but she persisted. For years. I never told her that most of her letters went into the rubbish bin, but she'd probably guessed that anyway. And still she wrote on, undeterred.

When I did respond it was usually out of self-interest. She would make an offer of some kind that I had an interest in, and I would respond.

Caroline Davis worked for *Reader's Digest*. Her signature appeared on all their promotional letters, at least in Australia. But I never kept them because they weren't personal, not even when they included my name. I knew her interest was in selling something. (Besides, she never kept her promise of huge rewards—even when I said yes to something she offered.)

The problem? Organisations can't be personal. And that's something even churches need to understand.

This is especially so when, every five years, the main focus of the church and church leaders is on the General Conference (GC) session. We may be tempted to think that during this time those involved have been doing church. No, they were doing church organisation.

The GC session is a 10-day showcase of the worldwide church. It's also a time for the election of GC officers and departmental staff, policy making and major discussion.

It's important and necessary.

But real church is not at the GC, the division, the union or even the conference levels: it's what happens locally. Real church is the Sabbath experience we share with others. It's the personal contact made in the community. It's the witnessing in the workplace. Real church is about building relationships.

The example, as always, is Jesus. He didn't need a publicist to make an impact. Sure, His miracles created interest, but there was also a personal touch that drew people to Him. He wept at the tomb; rejoiced at the wedding; partied with sinners; washed feet—that's when He said, "I have set you an example that you should do as I have done for you" (John 13:15).

"By this all men will know that you are my disciples," adds Jesus a little further on. But He doesn't emphasise excellence in organisational procedures, or dynamic institutions or first-class administration. They will know, says Jesus, "if you love one another" (John 13:35).

Real church is about a relationship with God, and a face-to-face relationship with others—which is often a check on the depth of the relationship with God. The challenge is to develop the kind of relationship with each other featured in 1 Corinthians 13. The attitudes in that chapter also make for winning witnessing.

Only individuals can do this. That was the weakness in Caroline Davis's letters. I knew she was really a front for a company; she had no personal interest in me.

We sometimes forget that the primary function of the various levels of church administration, institutions and organisation is to support the local church. Those other levels have a significant role to play in resourcing churches for nurture and evangelism, in providing big-picture strategies, being a reference point for teaching and procedures, providing institutional oversight etc. But they will never replace what happens in the local church.

Both are necessary. For instance, growth through Global Mission wouldn't happen without an organisational structure. But Global Mission would fail without Adventists from local churches being willing to give their time to help create other local churches. The Global Mission strategy demonstrates well a positive partnership between administration and the local church.

Good administration, good communication or a public relation's blitz will never replace personal contact. In fact, even after all the letters, I doubted if Caroline Davis was a real person. (Yes, she is; and, yes, she still works with *Reader's Digest,* but in a different area.)

I may be able to recognise Ms Davis's handwriting, but I wouldn't know her face—or anything else about her. Is she married? Does she have children? What are her hobbies? Did she cry at the end of the film, *Mr Holland's Opus?*

God became flesh and blood to demonstrate what He is like. And He uses flesh and blood to continue the demonstration. Technology, organisational ability and structure may help create interest or aid efficiency, but it's people-to-people contact in local churches that has the greatest long-term influence.

And it's in the local church where church really happens.

THE FRED PHELPS
SCHOOL OF EVANGELISM

Fred Phelps is a man with a mission. And it's a mission from God, he says.

When homosexual student Matthew Shepard was beaten to death in Wyoming in 1998, Fred Phelps came to town. He was shown on national media waving a picture of Shepard's face surrounded by blood-red flames and chanting, "Matt is in hell!"

This 70-year-old pastor of a small church travels the US with a message of hate. More often he's seen with signs painted in Day-Glo with messages such as "God hates fags" or "Fags are worthy of death."

He and his family particularly target churches that are pro gay, or have allowed homosexual "weddings." He also targeted the funeral of Bill Clinton's mother because, he said, she's related to "the evil one who corrupts from within the White House."

"It's a modern myth that God hates sin and loves the sinner," he told *Christianity Today.*

"The Bible preaches hate. For every one verse about God's love, mercy, and compassion, there are two verses about His vengeance, hatred, and wrath. What you need to hear is that God hates people, and that your chances of going to heaven are nonexistent unless you repent."

Let's agree about repentance, but the rest is a denial of John 3:16—no matter how he wants to do his maths. And it's a denial of John 3:17 where Jesus says He came to save the world, not condemn it.

But what about truth? Shouldn't we share the truth? No matter how unpopular the message might be? Even the Bible's message about homosexuality in a world that's increasingly pro gay rights?

Paul certainly counselled that we should speak the truth. Speak it in love, he said (see Ephesians 4:15).

Consider truth. We as a people promote biblical truth, which is as it should be. Obedience to truth has certain consequences. Notice: "Now that you have purified yourselves by obeying the truth so that you have sincere love for your brothers, love one another deeply, from the heart" (1 Peter 1:22).

I wish Fred Phelps could understand that.

Unfortunately the word *love* is usually viewed as a soft word linked to romance. Used in that sense, it's something you fall into, not something you build up. And it's something that's related to feelings, not to principles. But God, who governs according to principle, did demonstrate His feelings for us in that He so loved us, He gave Himself through His Son. But His love is broad—for the just and the unjust alike. His love is *the* example of self-sacrificing, other-centred love.

But there's more: consider the Holy Spirit. The Holy Spirit in your life means a development of the fruit of the Spirit. The fruit of the Spirit, Paul says in Galatians 5:22, is love (the word *fruit* is singular, pointing to love, *with* joy, peace, patience etc, flowing out of love).

Consider spiritual gifts. Here, Paul has a warning. You can have the highest of the gifts—prophecy, for instance. Or you can have the lowest of the gifts—tongues, for instance. Or you could even give your body as a martyr, but if you don't have love, it's worthless. That's the message of 1 Corinthians 13.

Jesus commanded us to love; He said it was His "new" command, adding that if we loved one another, that would be a sign of true discipleship (see John 13:34, 35).

That means there's no room in the church for petty division, for example, and that means some of us may have some apologising to do. Jesus' command certainly means there's no room in His church for graduates of the Fred Phelps School of Evangelism. We're called to show love, not hate.

John Paulk was one homosexual confronted by Phelps and his family as they chanted "God hates fags!" from the sidelines of a gay-pride parade.

"That made me fear Christians; that made them the enemy," he told the *Christianity Today* reporter. "It wasn't until I met a Christian couple who were willing to embrace me and love me first, that I began to listen to what they had to say about the way and the truth about homosexuality." (Paulk is now married with two children and works for the Christian organisation Focus on the Family.)

"It's easy to judge," Paulk says, "but it's hard to love. Their love earned them the right to speak to my life."

That's the power of love.

SWOOSH, FISH,
CROSS & U

March 1996. Nike sets a new standard for advertising. It deletes the word *Nike* from its logo. You're now expected to recognise the brand simply by its trademark swoosh (no, Nike will tell you it isn't a tick).

Nike figures its brand is so much a part of the world's culture that they can afford to drop the name.

The swoosh symbolises many things, says Nike. The wings of the goddess of victory (Nike). It's the last sound you hear before coming in second. It's the sound a basketball makes when it goes through the hoop and hits nothing but the net. Some suggest it even looks like the sound as you read the symbol from left to right.

One wonders if Caroline Davidson had any of that in mind when, as a university student, she designed it in 1971. She was paid $US35 by the then-professor Phil Knight who had this idea of importing running shoes.

Taking away the text was a brilliant move by Nike.

"By being textless, it transcends language and allows the viewer to understand it whether or not they speak English (or Greek)," says Read Schuchardt in "The mark of the best" (*Zadok Perspectives*, Autumn 1998). "With literacy on the decline, cultural pluralism on the rise and corporations producing more and more globally exported products, a communication medium that transcends language will always communicate more efficiently than one that is bogged down in actual words."

Schuchardt goes too far when he sees this as a demonstration that language is disappearing, to be replaced by sets of universal icons and heiroglyphs (shades of ancient Egypt). But maybe the pop star formerly known as Prince, who adopted a symbol for his name, was ahead of his time.

Symbols without text are now a part of our lives. Mercedes-Benz and Pepsi-Cola recently followed Nike's lead. Other lesser-knowns are experimenting.

Symbols aren't new. One of the earliest is from the Roman Empire—the Christian symbol of the fish. The symbol and the word both meant something. The Greek word *ichthus* (fish) became an acronym: *Iota*—*Iesous*—Jesus; *chi*—*Christos*—Christ; *theta*—*Theos*—God; *upsilon*—*huios*—Son (that is, Son of God); *sigma*—*soter*—saviour.

The fish symbol, with the acronym, became a statement of belief for Christians. Under Roman oppression, it became the secret, textless sign to indicate you were a believer, and a sign of safety for fellow believers. It's a sign still found in the catacombs of Rome.

And, of course, the cross is a worldwide symbol of Christianity. It's textless, and in some nations it has power, for it indicates a Christian presence where most follow a different faith.

Unfortunately, the cross holds little meaning in the Western world, except as a signpost for some church buildings. It's more likely to be seen as jewellery, and that may only mean the person wearing it likes the shape, or it's an heirloom with sentimental value, or there's some superstitious belief.

That's why God left something far greater than a symbol or icon as His marketing strategy. He left flesh and blood—you and me.

We have a message. It's the message proclaimed in the fish symbol of the second century. It's the message of the cross from the first century. And it's the message of Jesus' return for the 21st century.

But sometimes the message must be textless. There's not the opportunity to speak. That's when the life must reflect the belief in such a way that the belief is obvious.

"You were once darkness," says Paul, "but now you are light in the Lord. Live as children of light . . ." (Ephesians 5:8). And living as light in the Lord only adds power when we can add text.

Putting it another way, "The badge of Christianity is not an outward sign, not the wearing of a cross or a crown, but it is that which reveals the union of man with God. . . . The strongest argument in favour of the gospel is a loving and lovable Christian" (*The Ministry of Healing*, page 470).

JESUS IN
PINSTRIPES*

Hot Sabbath.
Cloudless sky.
City church shimmers.
Bright-coloured dresses.
Shirt sleeves.
Summertime church.

Holiday-time church.
Ushers struggle finding room
For family and friends visiting.
Extra chairs are filled.
Overhead fans wearily stir the air
As women flutter papers to cool themselves,
And men stoically melt.

Except for Brother Smitherton.
He always looks cool.
Summer or winter,
Winter or summer.
Always cool in his pinstriped suit.

The preacher battles
Teenage whispers
And heat-dulled minds
Preparing lunches
And holiday plans.

But not with Brother Smitherton
He always listens.
Summer or winter,
Winter or summer.
Always listens in his pinstriped suit.

"Brother Smitherton is a good man,"
Parents tell their children.
"He may seem a little strange,
A little old fashioned
And a little straight,
But he does what he thinks is right.
You should respect that."

No-one seems to notice
When the church door opens.
Then . . .

A gasp.
Heads turn.
The pastor freezes
In mid exegesis.
He splutters,
Pauses,
Adjusts his glasses
And continues.

SALT, NOT MUSTARD

But all attention is on
The one coming through the door.
Who is *he*?
A flowerchild from the '60s?
With hair and beard to match?
A biblical look
In sleeveless shirt
And ragged jeans.
A voice from the wilderness?
No, he sleeps behind the shopping mall.

Barefoot down the aisle
He looks for a seat,
But every pew is full.
Brother Smitherton gives a start
When he passes by,
And frowns in wonder at
The jeans, the shirt and hair.

There are no seats,
But he sits!
On the floor!
In the aisle!
Next to the front pew!

Whispers:
Indignant,
Questioning.
Laughter from the back.
The pastor adjusts his notes
And bravely reads a verse,
Only to stop . . .

He sees the pinstripes rise
And, with serious demeanour,
Black Bible pressed to breast,
Walk toward the front of the church

There's barely a breath
While the people wait
Expecting . . .
Expecting . . .
Not knowing what to expect.
So they watch as
Brother Smitherton sits
Next to him!
On the floor!
In the aisle!
Next to the front pew!

And he greets him like a friend
And opens his Bible
And shares it with him.

Smiles.
Smiles on a hot Sabbath.
A hot Sabbath
When the church discovered
Jesus in pinstripes.

*Based on a story by Tony Campolo.

NEXT DOOR TO
DAVID GRAY

David Gray was considered "different." The people of Aramoana, South New Zealand, discovered how different just a few weeks ago.

One evening he dressed in camouflage overalls, blackened his face, and pulled on a balaclava to go on a rampage in the streets of what had been a quiet town. For 23 hours he lived a fantasy built on images from the books and magazines he had devoured. After killing 14 people he died like some comic-book hero, with a defiant yell and guns blazing.

Newspaper reports say that people remember him as a misfit. Those at school with him remember him as tall and skinny. The children teased him because of his squeaky voice.

"He was weird," remembered a former classmate.

Some described him as emotionally immature, with an intelligence level below average. A former teacher said he was vulnerable and sensitive. He left high school before finishing, and eventually worked as a farmhand.

A former neighbour said, "You hardly ever saw him. He did nothing. His mum would mow the lawns, and he would stay in his bedroom."

He grew into an antisocial loner who seems to have had a chip on his shoulder.

"He made himself an outcast," said a Dunedin bookshop owner. "He hated women for some reason, and he saw society as bad."

"I don't think anyone really knew him," reported a resident of Aramoana. "He'd just walk up and down the street, and if you were on the same side he'd cross over before he reached you."

"People went out of their way to speak, but he brushed past," reported another. "No-one could engage him in conversation. You would only get a grunt."

No-one really knew David Gray. Even though some saw signs that he was capable of violence, none could have guessed that he would go on a killing spree. Only after the killing did anyone realise that he had a stockpile of eight rifles, and hundreds of rounds of ammunition stored with the milk in his fridge.

There are a lot of David Grays on this planet. Misfits. Loners. Few of them go so far as to kill others, but their problems are the same. They face a world that, to them, is hostile.

Jesus had a special ministry to the misfits. The woman at the well. Zaccheus. The woman caught in adultery. The lepers. These people were victims in a society that didn't care too much for those who were different. Sometimes their situation was their own fault; often it wasn't.

"'Which of these three [in the story of the good Samaritan] do you think was a neighbour to the man who fell into the hands of robbers?'

asked Jesus.

"The expert in the law replied, 'The one who had mercy on him.'

"Jesus told him, 'Go and do likewise'" (Luke 10:36, 37).

It's a command to be a good neighbour—even to the misfits.

Would it have made a difference to David Gray if someone had persisted in trying to get to know and understand him?

Maybe it would have made no difference. Maybe there were people who tried everything possible to help him. Maybe he was bent on a course of destruction and nothing would ever change that.

But there are a million other David Grays out there who will never be noticed except for their eccentric ways. They need friends who will be persistent in their friendship. They need to know about the God who cares for misfits.

Of course, developing that kind of friendship for the misfits may interrupt our social life. And it will take time.

But we're called to be salt to give the earth a certain taste. We're called to be light to brighten the dark places. We're called to show God to even the misfits.

The Aramoana tragedy reminds us of how far some people will go to get back at a world that seems to have rejected them. And it seems that this sense of rejection caused David Gray to do the unthinkable.

In this case, there may have been many who tried to befriend and help him, yet he rejected them.

The thing that haunts me about the David Gray story is this: Do I live next door to a misfit? Have I gone out of my way to find out? Would I make a difference?

THE OUTSIDER

"I want to tell you why there aren't many people joining the church today!" exclaims the voice.

"Really?" I reply. Maybe I'm cynical, but when someone claims to have *the* solution I have this "Oh yeah?" feeling deep inside. Besides, I don't need this—not today. I'm trying to meet deadlines that can't be extended. Maybe if I humour him he'll go away.

"Yeah. My name's ———. I read where you said that the church was only growing by 1.5 members per church. I know why it is."

"Tell me." I throw out the challenge. He's got a broad Australian accent, and he obviously thinks that what he's about to say is important. It's a long-distance phone call from interstate.

"You people won't accept anyone from outside your own group. You've got to belong to the Seventh-day Adventist Church before anyone within the church takes any notice of you."

"You're not an Adventist?"

"No. But my wife is. And *I* know the Adventist Church. And *you* need to know what happens to those on the outside.

"Look, my daughter goes to an Adventist school, and I'm happy about that. I've spent hours at the school on working bees and helping out. I've seen what happens—preference is always given to the church members. If you don't belong to the 'club,' you're on the outside.

"I've been to church functions a few times, and the same thing happens there. It's as if it's all relaxed until I turn up. Then there's a coolness—I can feel it. When one of the members turns up it's all friendly and backslapping and good-on-ya-mate. You've got to belong to belong, if you know what I mean?"

"Are you sure you're not just imagining that they're being cool toward you?" Here's my chance to defend the church.

"I know when I'm not wanted. This isn't the only Adventist church I've been associated with. It happens all over. If you belong, you're welcomed with open arms. If you don't belong, you're held at arm's length.

"Until you really *want* those outside the church to come inside they're not going to want to join the church. People just don't go where they're not wanted."

He emphasises the point. I'm starting to feel that anything I say isn't going to do much for the image of the church in his mind. But he's not finished.

"In all the years I've known the church I've only ever been invited to church once—and that was by the minister. If you were really serious about wanting to grow, surely you'd think that I would have had more invitations to the church."

What can I say?

We talk for a few more minutes. Then he hangs up. I'm left with my deadlines, an article waiting to be worked over, and a dozen other things I'm to do before I leave this evening.

In between keystrokes on the computer I try to rationalise away what I've just heard. I'm glad I don't attend the church he's referring to in ——. No, I won't tell you where. It might be your church.

On the other hand, it wouldn't be your church, or mine, would it? We'd be careful to watch out for those who don't seem to be fitting in. We'd try to make them as comfortable as we could. People would never go away from our church saying they weren't wanted.

Or would they?

It's easy to develop a club-like atmosphere at church in which we mix with the same people week after week, building a barrier between ourselves and those "out there." It becomes "us" and "them"—insiders and outsiders.

Maybe I should let —— make one more comment.

"Look, mate, I'm an outsider. You may not like what I'm telling you, but that's what's happening. The church needs to know it. It will never increase if it has that attitude."

But, as he says, he's only an "outsider." He doesn't know the warm fellowship we enjoy. We're comfortable.

Is the gospel commission important enough for us to risk becoming *un*comfortable?

ORDINARY SAINTS

ORDINARY SAINTS

Somehow across the centuries the concept has crept into the Christian church that you'll find saints on stained-glass windows or in books gathering dust on the shelves of dank libraries.

Too often we have perpetuated the idea that the only real saint is a dead saint.

Wrong!

Look around your church. That's where you'll find the saints. God's people are His saints.

A dead saint may have fought the good fight, may have stored up the crown, and may be awaiting the Second Coming. But other than providing inspiration for us, a dead saint has little value. Give me a living saint any time.

So am I seriously suggesting that the people in your church are saints? If your church is like the church I attend, it has some characters in it who don't seem to be too saintly.

But maybe we don't notice the saints because we expect a halo. I think you'll read of only two people in the Bible who glowed halo-like—Jesus and Moses. In reality saints are living, breathing, sweating humans like you and me.

Yes, I'm suggesting that the people who sit in the pews with you Sabbath by Sabbath are saints. And I'm suggesting that you also are one of God's saints.

When Paul wrote his letter to the Corinthians he called them saints ("sanctified ones," in some modem versions). But I don't know anyone who would want to be a member of the church board as they considered his letter.

In Paul's first letter to the Corinthians, almost every chapter condemns the church for some sin. There's immorality in the church. The members argue about whether they're Apollosites, Paulites or Cephasites. There are lawsuits going on between church members. They argue about food that has been offered to idols. Some question the doctrine of the Resurrection. Their Communion service has become a sham. Their worship service has become a free-for-all. And they have a problem with tongues-speaking.

You may think your church has problems. Corinth was every pastor's nightmare.

So did Paul get it wrong when he called them saints? If he did, he got it wrong twice. His follow-up letter is addressed "to the church of God in Corinth, together with all the saints throughout Achaia" (2 Corinthians 1:1).

He's obviously talking about a different kind of saint from those who have been canonised. You won't find too many listed on the Corinthian church roll who made it into stained glass.

Saintliness has more to do with relationship to Jesus Christ than with mere external acts.

Ellen White equates sainthood with conversion: "The eternal God has drawn the line of distinction between the saint and the sinner, between converted and unconverted" (*Messages to Young People*, page 390).

Every born-again person in your congregation is a saint. And they're much more effective as saints than the stained-glass variety. They know what it's like to face the struggles of the 21st century and still have a commitment to God—and that's more inspiring than halos.

Paul, Peter and others through the centuries were the saints of their day. They did great things for God, and we need to remember their deeds. However, most saints, of all ages, have been the ones we never hear about—the "nobodies" who were an unheralded part of the body of Christ doing their bit for Him.

It's the same today. Few have the gifts, the calling or the dedication to be a Mother Teresa, who was recognised by the popular press as "a saint of the gutter."

Most of God's saints are regular you-and-me-type people who have committed their lives to God. They're people just like the ones who sit in your church week after week. *God's people* are His saints—flesh and blood, working for Him.

To be canonised has no significance, really. Stained glass has only aesthetic value. Working toward that kind of sainthood may even be an obstacle to achieving the real thing.

Mind you, though, Saint Bruce does have a certain ring to it, doesn't it?

THOUGHTS ON
BRUCE ALMIGHTY

The title of the movie *Bruce Almighty* caught my attention. I guess it wouldn't have had the same impact if it had been named *Fred Almighty* or *Susan Almighty*. For a fleeting moment I wondered how a sign *Bruce Almighty* would go on my office door. But the concept of the movie got me thinking. And, no, I haven't seen the picture; I'm writing this the day *before* its release in Australia.

Christian film critics in the US, I notice, are divided about its value. I won't attempt to judge it, because I can't, and, besides, that isn't the point here.

The story is about Bruce Nolan (played by Jim Carrey), a self-centred man whom God calls into His office. God, if you've ever wondered, is American, black and (the feminists were wrong) male, and looks suspiciously like Morgan Freeman. God gives to Bruce His powers for a week—he becomes Bruce Almighty.

What would you do?

This is the point—if you were God, what would you do? If you were omnipotent, what changes would you make to our planet? Where would you start?

How about world hunger? How would you fix it? Food for everyone? How? Multiply loaves and fish, perhaps? Manna from the sky? Create a glut of food?

If you decide to go the miracle route, that of miraculously supplying food, is this a once-only situation, or will you plan to keep it going? And what are you going to do for the farmers who just lost their income? If you decide to create a glut of food, how will you get it across contested borders or to those in countries where they are oppressed? Through another miracle?

Miracles are fine and, if you're God, you can create one whenever you want. But if you decide to create a continuous miracle, how long does it go on for before it ceases to be a miracle and become an everyday event? What restrictions on human choice are set in place with a continuous miracle? And, if you are God, is there then a danger that people will begin to worship the miracle rather than God?

What about working on world peace? Where would you start? The Middle East? The civil wars in African nations? Or you could start simply—by fixing Iraq. And, remember, we want long-term peace.

What persuasion will you use? What promises? What are the trade-offs? Or will it take another miracle?

The Almighty Jesus

Only one human could add the word *Almighty* to His name and be true to its meaning—Jesus. Yet He didn't bother attempting to bring peace to the Middle East. Sure, He fed several thousand a meal or two, but it was short-term only. He had sympathy for the poor, but didn't supply a long-term solution, for "they will always be with you," He said.

Jesus, the real God-man, worked to a different agenda. He tackled the base problem, the condition of the human heart.

The frustrating thing about our planet is that world hunger, the lack of peace and poverty could be fixed if we humans would work together. Yet people go hungry because someone with authority—a warlord or bureaucratic contrivance—stops or tampers with the food supply. Peace breaks out in one place and war begins in another. And the poor remain poor for a variety of reasons.

The core problem is sin. Fix the sin problem, and the other problems are solved. This is what God Almighty worked on. Jesus is His response.

Why act as if we are God?

You won't find a sign saying "Bruce Almighty" on my office door. It smacks too much of—to use what seems to be considered an old-fashioned term—blasphemy. Yet how often do I—do we—act like we are God?

It happens when we act as if the world revolves around us. As if we're immortal. As if we know everything and have all the answers. As if we can tell God what to do. Even in our Gethsemane experiences, we like to ask God to fix the problem but have in mind how. This is the same as praying, "Not Thy will but mine be done!" When I do that, I act as if I'm Bruce Almighty.

Let's allow God to be God. Let's allow Him to work His wonders in and through us as we wait for Him to bring the final resolution of all problems on this planet. And let's remind ourselves that the "poor in spirit" are the ones who receive the kingdom (Matthew 5:3).

THE ULTIMATE
REALITY

In the past, warfare was with weapons that "knocked off the enemy, one by one." Even in ideological warfare of the past—the 18th and 19th century—proceeded to convince by "persuading individuals to adopt new points of view, one at a time."

"Electric persuasion by photo and movie and TV works, instead, by dunking entire populations in new imagery." Put the quaintness of "electric persuasion" down to the fact that this was written in 1964 by Marshall McLuhan in his, at times, prophetic book *Understanding Media*.

McLuhan is perhaps best known for the concept of the world as a "global village." That term was first coined in this book. He could see the media drawing the world together to create this village.

McLuhan came to mind as I *watched* the Iraq war unfold on television. Think about that sentence. I watched the Iraq war unfold on television. We were spectators to a war. For the first time, we were "embedded" with troops as they went to battle. Wherever the troops were, cameras were; wherever cameras were, we were.

Big Brother, *Survivor* and *Temptation Island* may call themselves "reality TV," but the war in Iraq was the ultimate in the reality genre. The bombing, the killing, the bodies, the weeping, the anger, the joy, the pain—all real.

A bomb goes off near a convoy and a cameraman's blood spatters onto his television lens. *This* is reality TV.

We ate our evening meal as we digested the news of the day. We discussed what happened for us during the day in the ad breaks. Then we returned to watch experts second-guess what would happen next as images of war played in the background.

Yet we weren't getting the full picture. The media can't do that. It has two problems: the first is its limited view, and the second is the spin placed on the story by the presenter, producer or editor—whether it's intended or not.

The media itself becomes a weapon.

Watching Western TV, it seemed ludicrous that Iraqi Information Minister Muhammad Said al-Sahhaf would bother to deny the obvious when American troops were battering down doors in Baghdad. That wasn't the point. Television and the media was his weapon to hold the Iraqi troops and people behind Hussein's regime. The facts probably would have had the opposite effect.

He well understood the use of media to build an impression, to promote a cause. Television, in particular, is an ideal tool for this.

McLuhan tells the story of Archimedes who, in a discussion of levers and fulcrums, once said, "Give me a place to stand and I will move the world." "Today," wrote McLuhan, "he would have pointed to our electric media and said, 'I will stand on your eyes, your ears, your nerves, and your brain, and the world will move in any tempo or pattern I choose.'"

Television is a huge tool to persuade, but not for reality. The ultimate reality is not found on television, and it isn't what we witnessed in Iraq. The ultimate reality has good and evil battling for our planet. This is global, and broader than any media can depict. It reaches every nation. Every heart. Every mind.

Television gives glimpses, with evidences like Iraq, that this reality is in progress. But the reality isn't found on television—it's in the lives of individual Iraqis.

For Iraqis, the reality is that they can't turn off the pictures we saw on the screen; they're living with them—and the frightful ones we didn't see. They now have to rebuild lives out of rubble; they now have to overcome the grief of loss; they have to attempt to pull themselves together as a nation. They have to try to get back to the ordinariness of routine—something that doesn't make good reality TV, so it won't be done before the cameras.

For all of us, the reality of the great conflict between good and evil, between God and Satan impacts at various levels. Most isn't dramatic enough to make it to television screens. But that doesn't lessen the pain. So many live lives of quiet suffering. And there is frustration, untapped potential and a longing—a longing for something better.

What the war in Iraq does is remind us (as if we needed to be) of how much of the earth is scarred by the evil one. That reminds us that this is not what life should be like.

And that's a reminder of the promise that ends the Bible: "Yes, I am coming soon." We respond, "Amen. Come, Lord Jesus" (Revelation 22:20).

His return brings peace to a planet torn apart. The promise found in His birth, life, death and resurrection becomes reality at His second coming. This blessed hope ushers in a reality that's ultimate and introduces us to life that is, at last, really real.

SALT, NOT MUSTARD AND OTHER THOUGHTS ON BEING CHURCH

THE MIRACLE
OF LIFE

Reformed smokers and first-time grandparents fit into the same category—they can't stop talking about their experience. Recently I became a grandparent. Twice (twin boys—no, not identical). I find myself dropping them into the conversation, usually at the most inappropriate times.

First-time grandparents are worse than reformed smokers though; they have photographs. I've noticed that as people have looked at these photographs, they act as if you may think they're the best-looking babies they've ever seen. I can understand that. In fact, I've received some expert advice on the matter. At the time of birth, Ashton had decided he was comfortable where he was, thank you very much. His was a difficult birth and he spent a couple of days in the special-care ward, recovering.

When we visited him, there was a doctor checking him out. We chatted for awhile. He assured us that Ashton was doing fine.

"You know," says I, breaking into the conversation, "as I look around the ward here, I think he's the best looking one here."

He looked at me for a moment, then at Ashton.

"I think you're right."

He's a professional—that's his professional opinion. Or had he met grandfathers like me before?

Now, there are some negatives to becoming a grandfather. I've discovered two: You are suddenly married to a grandmother (which came as a bit of a shock, even though she is still the same, sweet woman). The other is, it makes you sound incredibly old.

Driving away from the hospital, it occurred to us that we had lived long enough to see a new generation of our family begun. That wasn't something we'd ever talked about before—there was a sense of satisfaction with the thought.

But the overwhelming feeling concerned the miracle of life. What parent is there who hasn't held their healthy newborn and contemplated the miracle they have in their hands? Those same feelings hit us when we first met Ethan and Ashton. It's part of the joy of new life.

And I thought about God.

In these moments, I think we gain a glimpse of how God views us. We're certainly the apple of His eye (Zechariah 2:10). More than that, not only were we created special, we're died-for special. We're His children, born again—there's the miracle.

One Friday our phone rang. The twins' mother was on the other end.

"Ethan just laughed," she said. That was the only reason for the phone call. (I haven't heard either of them laugh yet, but I'm assured they have. Currently I can go for about a week on a smile.)

And I see God calling heaven to a halt to point out what one of His children is doing. I see Him pulling out His photo album, or whatever recording means He has (the Book of Records, perhaps), and sharing the pictures there.

"Look how he/she has grown," He tells Gabriel.

Take a look at God's fridge! Plastered over it are crudely drawn notes in multicoloured crayons. Messages and pictures for God. Our prayers. Some of the letters in the words aren't quite right, because we don't know exactly how to say it right, to spell it right (see Romans 8:26). God becomes a stick figure, because we can't draw Him right; He's beyond our knowing.

That doesn't matter. His children take pride of place on His fridge. Or should I say, within His heart?

See the Father smile as His new-born-agains take their first stumbling steps. See Him help them back to their feet when they fall. See Him hold their hands as they try to run ahead of Him. See Him wrap His arms around them when they come running back. See Him challenge them with more complex tasks. See Him weep when we turn away from Him. See Him forgive.

See Him rejoice at the miracle in birth. And at the miracle of rebirth.

WHEN YOU WONDER
ABOUT GOD

Life hurts. Not every day. Not all the time, but the pain never seems to be too far away.

I remember the pain of a mother and her nine-year-old son as they clung to each other at a grave-side as the husband and father was buried. Surrounded by more than 100 people, they seemed incredibly alone. We, the family and friends who stood with them, could say nothing to ease their pain.

We were asking the same questions they were: Why? Couldn't God have done something?

There was a sense of numbness with the recognition of unfulfilled potential in the life gone, and of the struggle those nearest to him now have to face. It's a numbness that makes you wonder about God—whether He can be trusted.

Faith that challenges

We read the stories of Bible heroes and are awed by their faith. Try Hebrews 11: Noah takes God at His word and builds the ark; Abraham leaves hometown Ur for an unseen Promised Land; Moses leads the multitude out of Egypt. Then there's Elijah on Mount Carmel challenging the forces of evil. These are heroes of faith.

We still have faith heroes. Australian teacher Helen Hall fits that category—with sheer determination and faith that it was God's purpose, she built and ran a school for unwanted Karen refugees in Myanmar. And this against marauding armies, political chicanery and murderous threats.

While all who are Christians place their faith in God, most won't be faith heroes. Paul lists faith as a gift (see 1 Corinthians 12:9). Faith heroes have that gift.

Faith that just hangs on

At the other end of the faith spectrum is the faith that hangs on when everything seems to have fallen apart. I saw it in the life of a woman whose children were murdered. I remember attempting to give her consolation and encouragement. I came away encouraged by her attitude that while all may not be well on the earth, God was still in His heaven. Now, several years later, her faith in God continues, and continues to challenge me.

But even faith heroes go through low periods. A few days after his Carmel triumph, Elijah was hiding in the desert praying, "Enough, Lord. Take my life!" (see 1 Kings 19:4). He was still talking to God, believed He was there, but he could see no way forward.

How many times does David the psalmist picture this kind of faith? When he's not sure of the future; not sure of God's purpose, but he hangs on? And what of the father who asked Jesus to heal his son?

"Everything is possible for him who believes," said Jesus.

"Lord, I believe, help me overcome my unbelief" (see Mark 9:21-27). It was enough. It was faith building.

Faith that doubts

There are times of doubt. The classic example is the one who became known as the doubter—Thomas.

"Unless I see the nail marks in his hands," he said, "and put my finger where the nails were, and put my hand into his side, I will not believe it."

He wasn't prepared to trust the word of the other disciples. He wanted to see, to touch for himself.

A week later Jesus confronts him: "Put your finger here; see my hands. Reach out your hand and put it into my side. Stop doubting and believe."

The response? "My Lord and my God!"

"Because you have seen me, you have believed; blessed are those who have not seen and yet believed" (see John 20:25-29).

But we can see by considering the nail marks, the hands and the side of Jesus. We can see by considering the gift of God in Jesus. We can see by considering the life and death of Jesus. If you have a faith that doubts, get back to basics, back to Jesus.

It's Jesus who is the "author," "cause," "pioneer," "guide," "origin"; and "finisher," "completer," "perfecter," "end," "crown" of our faith (words used in various translations of Hebrews 12:2). The message is clear: He is the beginning and the end of our faith.

Faith that matters

It isn't the amount of faith we have that matters (a mustard seed's worth will do), but where we place it. Faith heroes, those just hanging on in faith and those at all stages in between, are called to put their faith in God. Even when we don't feel Him near, He is. Even through the valley of the shadow of death, He is with us. That's a promise.

THREE FUNERALS AND
A RESURRECTION

This week I attended a funeral. Nothing unusual about that. I've attended dozens of funerals; conducted a score or two as well.

A woman in her late 60s had succumbed to a 15-year battle with cancer. Those who knew her far better than I (I'd only met her a few times; we, my wife and I, are friends of one of her daughters) say her life had been an inspiration. And she faced her suffering with dignity and with courage.

An outgoing woman, she was heavily involved in church work. She had seen results for her witnessing.

"I came into the church because of her," one woman told me at the funeral. "I came to know her when we worked in the same office."

I tell you these things to remind you of something you already know: Life is three-dimensional. No matter how good, how broad the life-sketch painted during the funeral service, it can give only a one-dimensional picture. This woman had lived life to the full under what were at times trying circumstances. There was genuine sadness that she had now gone.

If you had been a dispassionate viewer of the funeral, it would have been just another funeral. (I was not, could not, did not want to be a dispassionate viewer. There were tears with and for the family at times. Are men allowed to admit that?)

And, you could say, funerals happen all the time. That would be true.

You could say the death was expected and thus, somehow, not as tough to face. But those who have been there know that's not the case. There's still the shock of loss, the pain in the parting.

I remember well—too well—another funeral. Etched into my mind is the sight of a father carrying a small white coffin from the back of the hearse to the grave site, his wife walking at his side. The baby had died after just a few days of life. I was expected to say something comforting and helpful. I can't remember what I said, but I do remember the sense of helplessness in the face of the enemy.

Death is the enemy.

Death is the enemy because we're designed to live. The Creator Himself breathed into humans the breath of *life*. When we're injured the body kicks in with an automatic healing process to bring us back to health—to make us more alive. We cling on to life—Tony Bullimore, the round-the-world sailor whose boat capsized between Australia and Antarctica, hung on in his upside-down yacht in freezing waters when the odds were totally, outrageously stacked against him.

We're designed to live. Otherwise every minor injury, every muscle pain and every emotional setback would have us curl up in a corner waiting to die.

It's OK to go raging into this night (to use a thought from Dylan Thomas) because death is not our original destiny. Death is an intruder.

Another death. This time a mother, a widow, watches her son die in a cruel, tragic way. Her son is a man who's had life experience, but his life has been cut short. She can do nothing but watch him slowly die. Do nothing but be there. His last concerns are for her.

She buries him and faces the darkness of despair.

But wait! With the dawning of Sunday comes news that something has happened. Resurrection? Could it possibly be?

Yes! The enemy has been conquered.

And Jesus is called the firstfruits—that means there's more to come. Listen: "As in Adam all die, so in Christ all will be made alive" (1 Corinthians 15:22).

Because of the resurrection of Jesus, what we hear at funerals about new life beyond the grave is more than just an empty promise designed to comfort the gullible. Jesus' resurrection makes the promise a reality. The parting is temporary for those in Christ.

What hope. What joy. What a promise. Hear the promise: Jesus has "destroyed death and has brought life and immortality to light through the gospel" (2 Timothy 1:10).

We're designed to live. That's our true destiny. Death may gain a temporary victory, but the trumpet will sound, the dead will rise. By God's grace, dead or alive, that will be the moment when we realise our true destiny—life eternal, with Him.

Insert the "Hallelujah Chorus" here.

RABBI FRED'S
SECRET OF SUCCESS

"I'm Fred; who are you?"

There was a gentle American accent in the voice. He looked to be in his late 50s, bald with a brief beard to compensate. His dark suit said business.

I'd just boarded an evening flight, AN 49, from Sydney to Melbourne and was hoping for a quiet trip home. I wasn't in talking mode.

We exchanged pleasantries. He asked what I did; I told him. I asked what he did. He immediately—eagerly—reached for his business card.

I began to regret requesting a window seat. He was looking more like a passenger from a nightmare, and I had no escape. Mentally I steeled myself, preparing to hear his life story, or of his business conquests—or failures.

But I was wrong.

It turned into one of the most interesting flights I've ever had. So much for first impressions.

Fred is the president of a management-consultant organisation, based in Phoenix, USA. He lives and has an office in Christchurch, New Zealand. He flies to Phoenix every six weeks to check his mail. He was in Australia working with AMP for a week or so. (*So what he was doing in economy class?*)

"Christchurch is the best city in the world, so why not live there?" he enthused.

Meals were served; he showed a great deal of interest in mine. I'd ordered kosher. (For those who actually like airline cuisine, you get twice as much. But there's a downside for vegetarians, because there's a 50-50 chance of being served a meat dish.)

"What have you got there?" asked Fred.

"Kosher."

"You can get kosher on this flight."

"Yes, this is a kosher meal."

I hunted out the card that said the meal had been prepared under the care of a rabbi. He looked at it for a moment, then handed it back.

A few minutes later he asked if he could see the card again. This time he took a pair of reading glasses from his top pocket and read the card.

"This is a kosher meal," he said. I agreed, and he gave the card back.

"I'm a rabbi, you know."

I didn't. And it took me a moment to adjust to the thought. A rabbi named "Fred" didn't fit any preconceived idea I'd ever had. But I had to admit, there did seem to be a Jewishness about him.

"What makes a rabbi?" I asked. It was the only question that easily came to mind.

"Six years of training and six languages," he responded. (He made it sound simple.)

The conversation drifted back to his work as a consultant. He works mainly with sales people (and often it's super-sales people, earning half a million dollars and more a year). He helps them work out career paths. He defined "career path" as the route to achieving whatever it was that they wanted from life; it didn't relate only to their work. In fact, he said, these people are usually so successful as far as work goes, they're looking for fulfilment in other areas.

Sometimes it does involve money goals. He told me how he helped a group of people plan to double their income within 12 months. He said the 12 months wasn't up yet and they had already achieved that goal.

He had my attention.

"What's the secret?"

At 30,000 feet, high above Canberra, Rabbi Fred told me his secret of success.

"I get them focused on what they do. I help them to get rid of the things they don't need to do, so they can concentrate on what they *want* to do.

"I help them have one day a week where, when they get to the end of it, they can rate it as 10 out of 10. It's the point when they can't think of anything else they'd rather have done with the day."

Again, he made it sound simple.

"Then," he added with a smile, "I help them work out how they can have five 10-out-of-10 days a week."

And just in case I'd missed the point, he added, "You see, the real secret of success is focus."

Wait a minute! Rabbi Fred was sounding remarkably similar to another rabbi centuries earlier. This rabbi said, "Let us throw off everything that hinders and the sin that so easily entangles, and let us run with perseverance the race marked out for us. Let us fix [focus] our eyes on Jesus, the author and perfecter of our faith . . ." (Hebrews 12:1, 2).

Focus may be the secret of success for life in general, but it is certainly so in the Christian life.

PARABLE OF
THE TWO PARENTS

It seems to me that God has put us who bear his Message on stage in a theatre . . . (1 Corinthians 4:9, The Message).

Once there were two parents. One was the parent of Roger; the other the parent of Stewart. Both sons were in the second year of school.

And lo, it was the time of the school play.

Roger and Stewart had lines to learn, and a role to play. The parent of Roger sat with him in the lounge room and helped him go over and over his lines. The parent of Stewart listened as she cleaned the house and prepared a nutritionally correct dinner.

The two parents attended the rehearsals to encourage their child. They both wanted to support them in their endeavours.

And it came to pass that at a certain point in the play, both Roger and Stewart forgot their lines. Before the teacher could share the lines, the other children did snigger, and they did laugh. While the teacher brought them back to order, both boys ran off the stage, trying to hide their tears as they ran.

The two parents hurried from where they sat in the hall, observing the rehearsal, to the back of the stage to give comfort and counsel.

The parent of Stewart knelt down beside him, held him at arm's length and told him in a voice heard by others in the hall, "I told you, you should have learned those lines better. Come on, I'll take you home. You need to practise some more."

The parent of Stewart heaved a sigh, shook her head and tsk-tsked several times as she walked out the door. Stewart had to run to keep up with his parent. And he found it difficult to see because of the tears.

The parent of Roger also knelt down. But she didn't say anything. She held Roger close and stroked his hair as she listened to the angry words Roger spoke.

Then, with her finger, she brushed away the tears on Roger's face.

She, too, held her child at arm's length. She spoke quietly to him and then said, "Come on, I'll take you home so we can practise some more."

The parent of Roger held his hand as they walked together to the door.

Again the two parents assisted in learning for the play. The parent of Roger sat in the lounge room and listened and corrected Roger when it was necessary to do so.

The parent of Stewart listened as she sat at the kitchen table writing a shopping list. She encouraged Stewart when he stumbled. "Get it right, boy!" and, "Look, these lines are not that difficult" were among the exhortations she used.

The two parents also assisted their boys in practising the comings and going involved in the school play, for they both had active roles.

The parent of Roger said, "Come, let me play the role of Tamara so that you can practise as if she were here."

As they did. Roger practised coming into the lounge room as if he were walking onto the stage. His parent spoke the words of Tamara and did indeed act as if she were the person Tamara. After he had said his lines, Roger left the lounge room as if he were leaving the stage.

Then they did it again and again until Roger said it was enough.

Stewart asked his parent if she would help him practise his comings and goings. The parent of Stewart took unto herself the role of Judith.

Stewart entered the kitchen as if he were coming onto the stage. His parent read the words of Judith. After he had said his lines, Stewart left the kitchen as if he were leaving the stage.

"See, that went well," said the parent of Stewart. Then she dismissed Stewart, for she had matters of a budgetary nature concerning her shopping list and a party she was planning on her mind.

The two parents returned for the rehearsal on the morrow.

At one point in the play Roger did forget his coming onto the stage. And the children did laugh once more. And Roger did cry.

The parent of Roger was quickly at his side. She held him close and whispered words of encouragement to him.

Roger determined to try again.

And then it was that Stewart did forget his going from the stage. And the children did laugh again. And Stewart did cry.

The parent of Stewart explained to the others in attendance that Stewart had got it right at home, and that she didn't know why he couldn't get it right on stage.

She took Stewart's hand with vigour and told the teacher in charge that she would enforce Roger to practise at home. She made fervent promises that all would be right on the night.

Then she encouraged Stewart with loud words as they exited through a side door.

Those who saw these things marvelled in their minds and questioned among themselves, "Which of these two is the Good Parent?"

HOW GOES THE BATTLE?

When my father died a few years back I inherited some of his books. Included among them was a well-worn copy of *Steps to Christ*. In fact, it was a copy he had during World War II.

On the cover is an American and an Australian flag with the words "The Services Edition." Inside he had written his name and rank and that he served with the 12th Australian Army Troops, with the engineers, in Rabaul (Papua New Guinea).

The book is soft covered and a little tattered, but after 60 years it has held together remarkably well.

It was quite a moving experience to read, for my personal devotions over a couple of weeks, my father's wartime copy of *Steps to Christ*. This was made the more moving because he had underlined sentences and passages that were significant to him.

Like many who have served during war, he never talked much about his experiences.

I can remember from my teenage years an old, ankle-length army coat he would wear on cold mornings as he went fishing. (He worked as a professional fisherman from the age of 12.) He would point to some holes in the coat and tell how these were bullet holes from when he single-handedly pushed the enemy off Shaggy Ridge—a site of heavy fighting in Papua New Guinea during the war.

We would remind him that the holes looked suspiciously like moth holes. Besides, if he had accomplished what he claimed, it would have changed the face of warfare forever. He served as a noncombatant.

I once had the opportunity to briefly visit Rabaul, where there are still many reminders of the war. I now have a mental picture of Dad there, probably on a nearby beach (where else would a fisherman go?), reading his *Steps to Christ*.

One day (was it there? on *that* beach?) he underlined a sentence: "The warfare against self is the greatest battle that was ever fought" (page 43).

He knew about war. He was there. He was involved in the war that mobilised the greatest number of men and women ever. Yet he recognised the truth concerning an even more vital war, the one within.

It's the spiritual conflict that Martin Luther referred to when he said, "I am more afraid of my own heart than of the Pope and all his cardinals."

"To remove the stains of sin requires the work of a lifetime," said Ellen White. "Every day renewed efforts in restraining and denying self are needed. Every day there are battles to fight and victories to be gained. Every day the soul should be called out in earnest pleading with God for the mighty victories of the cross" (*Testimonies for the Church*, Vol 4, page 429).

The classic statement of the conflict within is made by Paul in Romans 7. He knows what he wants to do, what he ought to do; but so often he lets himself down. "For in my inner being I delight in God's law; but I see another law at work in the members of my body" (Romans 7:22, 23).

He powerfully pictures the conflict as one over his sinful nature. And because this is a spiritual battle, it needs a spiritual answer—but not from within.

"Who will rescue me from this body of death? Thanks be to God—through Jesus Christ our Lord!" (Romans 7:24, 25).

He then continues, in chapter 8, to tell of the victories available to those who live the Spirit-filled life.

Each of us face this struggle. For each of us the battle rages, but there's also growth and maturity as we remain in Christ. And in Christ there is no condemnation (Romans 8:1). In Christ we are God's children and heirs to His glory (Romans 8:16, 17). In Christ, God is for us, so who can stand against us? (Romans 8:31). In Christ we are more than conquerors (Romans 8:37).

"Who shall separate us from the love of Christ? . . . [Nothing] will be able to separate us from the love of God that is *in Christ* Jesus our Lord" (Romans 8:35, 39, emphasis added).

The struggle is real, but the news is good. The battle is won as long as we remain firm in Him.

My dad? He was a victor in the "greatest battle that was ever fought."

HOW FAR
FROM EDEN?

They codenamed it Trinity. On July 16, 1945, it lit up the New Mexico (USA) desert.

The test was "successful beyond the most optimistic expectations of anyone," wrote General Leslie Groves. Groves was in charge of the top-secret Manhattan Project to develop the atomic bomb, the most destructive invention ever.

Trinity. The real trinity—the Father, Son and Holy Spirit—had displayed creative power. The US scientists demonstrated that they had found the secret to dismantling creation. And not with a whimper, but a bang.

Shock waves from that first blast broke a window some 200 kilometres from ground zero. Shock waves from the explosion three weeks later, at 8.15 am on August 6 some 600 metres above Hiroshima, changed the world.

"Thank God for the atomic bomb" read the headline of an article in *The New Republic*. The joy and the relief among the Allies was real. The war would soon be over. Thousands of Allied lives would be saved.

There was relief among the administration of the US government as they finally saw results for the $US2 billion investment (a lot of money in the 1940s) they had made in the bomb.

And God wept.

"The target is a purely military one," said US president Harry Truman. Yet some 70,000 men, women and children, mostly non-military, died instantly in the holocaust. Another 130,000 died over the next few months from radiation poisoning and burns.

Three days later another 70,000 lay dead or dying in Nagasaki. Among them were 250 Japanese soldiers (another military target?) and about the same number of Allied prisoners of war. Ironically this bomb exploded directly above the largest Christian cathedral in the Far East.

Now, 60 years on the pictures remain, haunting us. To remind us. To remind us of the stomach-churning reality.

"Nobody there looked like human beings. . . . There were people barely breathing trying to push their intestines back in. People with their legs wrenched off. Without heads. Or with faces burned and swollen out of shape. The scene was a living hell," remembers one Hiroshima survivor (quoted in Haruko Taya Cook and Theodore F Cook, *Japan at War: An Oral History*).

Were there other options to the atomic bomb, to end the war? Yes. Were they better options? Probably.

The images from Hiroshima have helped with the push for peace through the years. And those who defend the bomb as a deterrent to war do have a point. Having seen its power, there has been a decided reluctance to use this ultimate of weapons,

But the fear remains that one of the 20-or-so nations who have access to nuclear power will actually use (or develop for use) a bomb. Any modern nuclear weapon is many times more powerful than that dropped on Hiroshima.

Is it any wonder that people marched for peace in cities around the world during the 50th anniversary of the Hiroshima bombing? Is it any wonder that people are calling for the French to stop their planned nuclear tests in the Pacific?

No-one really expects that the pleas from Hiroshima survivors for a nuclear-free planet will be realised.

Tom Ferebee—the bombardier on the B-29 bomber *Enola Gay*, who dropped the bomb on Hiroshima—supports their call. Interviewed during the 50th anniversary, he said he has never felt guilty about his role. But he did say that thinking about his part in it was easier when Kermit Beahan was alive. (Beahan, who died in 1989, was the bombardier who dropped the bomb on Nagasaki.)

It was easier while Beahan was alive, said Ferebee, because there were two of them who had dropped atomic bombs.

"Now I'm the only one in the world," he added. "It should stay that way."

And it will. Unless . . .

One thing history teaches us is that a repeat of the Hiroshima tragedy is possible. If the Hiroshima images teach us anything it's this: We need a Saviour.

BUT . . .

An unusual thing happened on the way to the Exodus.

At 40, Moses had been set to conquer all of Egypt to help the Israelites. He was more than happy to kill a few Egyptians on the way. Perhaps he saw himself as another Joseph, saving his people.

Then comes the 40 years in the desert—and time for reflection. The bush—which isn't burning although it's burning—disturbs his quiet life.

God calls.

Moses answers.

"**But**, who am *I*, that *I* should go?" Good question. Who *is* he?

Well, he'd been brought up in the household of the world's most powerful ruler. He'd been trained in the world's greatest university. He'd learned discipline of the world's greatest army. And he'd practised diplomacy in the world's greatest government.

Yet suddenly he acts like a nobody—a shepherd from the backblocks.

"I'll be with you," God replies.

"**But**, who are *you*? When they ask me who sent me, what shall I tell them?" Another good question.

"Tell them the 'I AM' has sent you." Interesting answer.

"I AM" is always present. "I AM" is never "I was" or "I will be." It doesn't matter whether we consider the past, the present or the future, "I AM" is constant.

God is the "I AM" of Abraham, Aaron and Amos. The "I AM" of Joseph, James and John. The "I AM" of today, tomorrow and two millennia ago.

In a world of change, when the certainties of tomorrow are as fleeting as shadows, the "I AM" remains the same.

There's your answer, Moses. And maybe it's worth noting another truth: If God (the "I AM") is on your side, who can stand against you?

"**But** what if they don't believe me, and say, 'The Lord didn't really appear to you'?"

"What do you have in your hand, Moses?"

"A staff."

"Throw it on the ground.

"Why are you running away, Moses? Don't be frightened. Come back and pick it up—by the tail, of course.

"This is so that they'll believe that the God of their fathers has appeared to you. Now, put your hand inside your coat."

What's the point? God's miracles are a demonstration that when God calls He also gives the power to carry out the assignment. The familiar adage "God's bidding is His enabling" is true. Guaranteed the power of God, Moses is told to follow His bidding.

"**But** I won't know what to say. I've never been eloquent. And You know I can't think quickly when I'm under pressure."

"Moses, who gave you your mouth? Now go. I'll help you speak, and I'll teach you what to say."

But, "Can't You send someone else, please?" It comes as a final plea.

Isaiah heard the voice of God calling, "Whom shall I send? And who will go for us?"

Isaiah responded, "Here am I. Send me!"

Moses' response? "Here am I. Send Aaron!"

It's always easier to be up in the stands cheering than to be out on the field in the rough-and-tumble of the game. And it's always easy to say that someone else can do the task better.

But God hadn't asked someone else. He'd asked Moses—not only to get into the game, but to captain the team.

Yes, an unusual thing happened on the way to the Exodus. Very unusual.

Moses reluctantly returned to Egypt. He requested an audience with Pharaoh. And He let Aaron do the talking.

But by the third visit to Pharaoh, Moses was doing his own talking. He was beginning to fill the role for which he had been born. He was becoming the leader God wanted him to be.

What concerns me, though, is that the excuses Moses offered sound rather modern. We're still using them.

PETER

He'd failed. He knew it. Anyone watching him walk out of the courtyard knew it. His head hung low and his shoulders shook as he choked on freely flowing tears.

Peter could hear the words of Jesus as an echo in his mind, "Before the cock crows, you will disown me three times" (Matthew 26:75).

Not only had he said he didn't know Jesus, he'd said it with curses and oaths—words he hadn't used since his fishing days.

He'd failed, and he wasn't used to that, either. Sure, there were times when he'd done the wrong thing. He knew he sometimes spoke before thinking things through. But this was different.

He feared they'd kill Jesus. If they did, how could he make up for what he'd done?

He stumbled on in darkness. He didn't notice the promise of a new day on the horizon. The shadow over his heart hid it all.

He felt a fool. "Lord, I am ready to go with you to prison and to death" (Luke 22:33). Hollow words now. He couldn't even tell a servant girl that he followed the Nazarene. If the ridicule of a few people outside the courthouse worried him, how did he dare think he could lay down his life for Jesus?

The day had turned into a nightmare. In a trance he followed along the road to Calvary. He made no protest. No outcry. No reaching for a sword in some vain, symbolic gesture to try to stop the Crucifixion.

He watched numbly as they nailed Jesus to the cross.

Sabbath came. Bitterness and regret darkened the day. Tears fell. Somehow he had to try to get his life back together.

Jesus' words came to mind: "I have prayed for you, Simon, that your faith may not fail. And when you have turned back, strengthen your brothers" (Luke 22:32).

But he'd failed. How could he turn back? It was too late. Jesus had died. It was all over.

When the women came back so quickly on Sunday morning the disciples were certain that they'd been overcome with grief. They hadn't been able to find the tomb. Maybe they'd hallucinated an angel into being.

Or someone had taken the body. Or they'd misunderstood the message of the gardener. Or . . .

Peter had to look for himself. He ran. Forget about dignity. Forget about pride.

Maybe . . . It was barely thinkable. Yet he'd witnessed the Transfiguration. Jesus was a miracle worker. Could He perform the ultimate miracle? Peter pushed past John to go inside the tomb.

It was empty.

"Do you love me?" They stood on the shore of the Galilee together again. It was like old times, but it wasn't old times. Nothing could erase the happening of the past few days. The words hurt.

Three times He asked the question. Three times Peter responded. Then Jesus said, "Follow me!" (John 21:19).

Three years before on the same stretch of beach Peter had heard the same words, and had accepted the challenge to follow the Messiah. Again he followed His Saviour.

Peter became a new man.

"He had been converted; he was distrustful of self, and no longer a proud boaster. He was filled with the Holy Spirit, and through its power he had become firm as a rock, courageous, yet modest, in magnifying Christ. He was ready to remove the stain of his apostasy by honouring the name he had once disowned" (*The Story of Redemption*, page 251).

Now there were no apologies for his faith. Never again would he deny his Lord. He had a faith worth defending.

In another city Peter had another cross waiting for him. It had his name on it. But he was ready for it because he now had a faith worth dying for.

The difference was that he had met the crucified and risen Christ.

NEVER DROPPING
OUR ARMS

NEVER DROPPING OUR ARMS

Jesus wasn't the Messiah they wanted. The politically correct, religious establishment of His day soon discovered He went about mixing with the wrong people. He talked to sinners; He ate with tax collectors—those quislings who sold out their nation to fill Rome's coffers; and prostitutes left their patrons to follow this Man.

He touched lepers; He told of a *good* Samaritan (that was a new thought for most Jews); and He healed on the Sabbath in a startling demonstration of true Sabbath-keeping.

But Jesus was the Messiah they *needed*. That we need. He threw down the barriers of position, race and gender. He was a living demonstration of the inclusiveness of the "whosoever" of John 3:16. That *whosoever* included the religious leaders, tax collectors and prostitutes.

There is equality before God.

Desmond Tutu, Archbishop of Cape Town, challenged apartheid in South Africa on the basis of the equality he found in the Creation story of Genesis. Humans were created in the image of God. All humans.

"A sign that this account is actually inspired by God," claimed Tutu, "is the fact that it says that every human being is created in the image of God. It is an incredible assertion that you and I, whoever we may be—it has nothing to do with status, it has nothing to do with race—were made in the image of God. It is of universal application to every human being. . . . This saying is dynamite in any situation of injustice and oppression . . ." (Samantha Trenoweth, *The Future of God*).

But Jesus was also an example. We may *speak* of loving the sinner and not the sin—Jesus demonstrated the reality. See Him handle the crowd who brought the woman caught in adultery. Listen to what He says when He finishes writing on the ground (see John 8:10, 11): "Woman, where are they? Has no-one condemned you?"

"No-one, sir."

"Then neither do I condemn you. Go now and leave your life of sin."

She is accepted; her sin isn't. Where she expected condemnation, she found Someone who recognised her value as a person.

Was Jesus soft on sin? No.

Elisabeth Kubler-Ross tells of a man with AIDS who attended one of her seminars for the dying. He spoke to the group of growing up in a fundamentalist Christian home—with a family that believed AIDS was a punishment from God.

He told of how he knew he was homosexual even though he tried not to be. His family called the religious community to pray over him—a public experience that humiliated him. Everyone in his small town now knew about him, and many pointed him out in the street and laughed as, mocking, they said they wanted to pray for him too.

He left home, swearing never to return. After a time he contracted AIDS. In hospital and dying, his thoughts returned to his home. He remembered the bad times, but he also remembered good times. He determined to go home. One last time.

After years of no contact, he phoned home. He told his mother he was in hospital—dying of cancer, he said. He explained he needed to come home to say goodbye.

As he walked across the meadow to his old home, it was as if time had stood still, for nothing had changed.

His mother saw him and dropped everything to greet him. Then his dad saw what was happening and raced to catch up with her. At that moment all those bad memories, the nightmares, all fell away—and all he felt was a sense of incredible love.

He stumbled on toward them. His mother stretched out her arms. But then . . .

Fear.

When she sees my face she'll know; she's going to stop and drop her arms, he thought.

He stumbled on, bracing himself for rejection. Then they were in each other's arms. She hadn't stopped.

They stood there, cheek to cheek. And his mother whispered in his ear, "Son, we know you have AIDS, and it's OK with us."

The One hurt most by our poor life-choices whispers in our ear, "I know what you are, and that's OK." Then He goes a step further, "And here's how I can help you."

And we followers of Jesus are left with the challenge of never dropping our arms to another.

WHERE ARE THE
BIG-IDEA PEOPLE?

Bill Bright died on July 19, 2003, leaving an incredible legacy. He was founder of Campus Crusade for Christ, which now serves in 191 countries, with a staff of 26,000 full-time employees and more than 225,000 trained volunteers.

Impressive? Even more impressive are his two simple ideas, which may have had more impact for evangelical Christianity in the past 50 years than any other.

In 1956 he wrote a booklet, just a few pages long, entitled *The Four Spiritual Laws*. In it, he describes the sin problem and how a person can come to Christ. A basic primer for Christianity, it is the most widely disseminated religious booklet ever. It has been printed in 200 languages and distributed to more than 2.5 billion people.

Then, in 1979, he commissioned the film *Jesus*, a feature-length documentary on the life of Christ. *New Life* reports it has been viewed by more than 5.1 billion people in 234 countries—the most widely viewed and translated film (into more than 800 languages) in history.

Two simple ideas, but with a big impact for God.

People with a cause

I remember interviewing Sister Helen Prejean, a Catholic nun from the United States. She has a cause. She discovered her cause when asked to visit a man waiting on death row in a Louisiana prison. She has now accompanied five men to their state-sanctioned deaths.

She wrote of her experience in the book *Dead Man Walking*. That was then adapted into an Oscar-winning film. Sister Helen was in Australia for the opening performance of an opera of the same name, staged by the State Opera of South Australia in Adelaide.

She wants to end the death penalty in the US—one of only a handful of countries to retain this punishment option. Her biggest argument against the death penalty is to draw aside the curtain and allow people to understand the reality of what happens when the convicted person is killed.

Hers is a cause worth fighting for. She's rehearsed the arguments: the black and the poor have little chance of a reprieve, the white and wealthy almost always do; DNA testing has shown many incorrect decisions; it costs more to execute a person in the US (with the court processes and special prison arrangements) than to imprison them for life; and more.

Besides those reasons, she says, "We can't turn over to governments, which you can barely trust to fill a pothole and get the street right, to decide about human life." And, "I think God is on the side of life."

People making a difference

Today I visited ADRA Corner. This is a successful op-shop that raises funds for community needs. It's ideally placed on a five-ways crossroad, a roundabout along the Warburton Highway a few minutes drive from Melbourne's outermost eastern suburbs. It's well known and patronised by local and not-so-local residents.

But it's the story of Ray and Marion Jull that interests me. This couple wanted to make a difference in their retirement years. With an idea in mind, they found this closed-down shop with a house attached and sold their own home to buy the complex—to live in the house and open an op-shop, ADRA Corner—as their service to others.

Both are former teachers, and Ray is a skilled handyman who enjoys tinkering and fixing things. The op-shop keeps him busy. This is their helping gift to the community, supplying clothing and other goods to those who are struggling, but the funds raised also help people who are suffering. They are making a difference.

Big-idea people

These are big-idea people. And we need more big-idea people: those with ideas that impact for God in a mighty way; those who find a cause worth fighting for; and those who know how to make a difference.

But we of lesser ideas also have a role. We are the encouragers of those who think big, to be supportive, to allow for the occasional failure, but with the encouragement that will let them try again.

I've worked with people who seem to have 10 ideas a minute (not all of them good—the ideas, that is). Sometimes our role is to help them tease out the good ideas, and that only happens if we're supportive of people with ideas.

We shouldn't always expect the church to have ideas for us. We're in a well-organised church, but structure and process don't always encourage big ideas. You'll notice with the ideas I've mentioned that they came not from organisations, but individuals. Thankfully, their organisations backed what they did, but individuals drove the ideas.

So let's encourage people with big ideas, and watch what God can do.

CRIPPLED
MINDS

Another crippled day
    for the man beside the
        pool.
A Sabbath.
It makes no difference,
    he's had thirty-eight years
        of crippled Sabbaths.
He waits, with the others,
    for the miracle that never comes.

"Do you want to be well?"
He looks toward the voice
    and wonders at the joke.
But the eyes aren't joking.
So he tells of waiting
    for a miracle that never comes;
    of waiting by the pool
        for thirty-eight years.

"Take up your bed and walk!"
Can He mean it?
Yet even with the question
    the Stranger's words
        strengthen his body.
New life flows into wasted legs.
New hope flashes through his mind.
He stands! He walks!
He runs! He jumps!

He runs beside the pool
    among those who await
        their miracle.
Thirty-eight years . . . just a memory.
He's now out of place . . .
    out of place
        among broken bodies.
He no longer belongs,
    not at the pool.

"Thank you! Thank you! Thank . . . !"
But the Stranger is gone.
He rolls up his mat
    and walks . . .
He walks!
He walks toward home.
His miracle has come.
He walks and runs and jumps.

Sabbath crowd by the temple.
He passes among them,
    barely noticing them there.
He's going home.
But they notice *him*,
    a springbok in the Sabbath herd,
    carrying his bed mat
        on the Sabbath day.

Angry voices slow his pace.
"Shame!" they cry.
"How dare you?" asks one.
"Have you forgotten . . .
    forgotten the Sabbath?"
Priests with thundered brows
    come toward the scene
        as fast as dignity allows.

"What are you doing?"
They pull rule books
    from their robes
        and flip them to the place.
"Look, page 2-2-3;
Subsection d;
Point i-v.
Can't you see?"

"But can't you see?
I couldn't walk and now I can!
I was a cripple till I met the Man."
"But you miss the point.
It's the Sabbath,
    and the law forbids
        you to carry your mat."

"But *you* miss the point.
I couldn't walk and now I can!
I was a cripple till I met the Man."

"But thou shalt not . . .
Thou shalt not run on the Sabbath.
Thou shalt not carry a load.
Thou shalt not laugh on the
    Sabbath.
Thou shalt not travel the road.
Thou shalt not . . ."

"But you miss the point.
I couldn't walk and now I can!
I was a cripple till I met the Man."

"Who told you to carry your bed?
    to break the Sabbath?
    to bring disgrace?
    to cause concern?"

"All I know is:
I was a cripple
    till I met the Man."
And he walks away.
Away from the men
    with crippled minds

Based on John 5:1-15.

JUST ANOTHER
MARRIAGE BREAKDOWN

"Last year, in October, my husband and I separated after almost 26 years of marriage. As you can imagine it has been a traumatic, soul-searching few months . . ."

So begins a letter to the editor.

That they support each other despite the separation is the good news. But there's also bad news.

"I've been extremely disappointed by the reaction of the church family. Separation can be likened to a death, because it is the death of a marriage. Unfortunately, it is not viewed like that by others, for I have not had one phone call or visit from anyone in the church where I have chosen to worship.

"If my husband had died, I would have been inundated with flowers, cards, food and offers of help. In this case, apart from my family and a few close friends, there is no support."

One of the tests of the church is how it helps individuals in a practical way during their times of greatest trauma. I don't know the church this woman attends, but reflect for a moment: if it were your church, would she suffer the same disappointment?

If she were to attend your church this Sabbath and you knew her story, how would she be received? And what about her husband?

"I understand that people don't know what to say and may even feel uncomfortable in my presence because of my situation. All I'm saying is that, right or wrong, I'm a human being who is hurting, and all I need is for *you* to take the time to show that you actually care."

For a number of years she supported her husband, who was employed by the church, both in the homeland and as a missionary's wife. She says she believes he was a more effective worker because of her presence.

In this way she supported the work and mission of the church. Now that she needs support, she's not finding it where she expected it. Sure there is some, from family, and from outside the church.

"My faith in Jesus as my Saviour is the only thing that sees me through some days, because humans have failed me. My family and a few close friends are the only ones who keep in touch.

"One of those friends—not a Seventh-day Adventist—has been closer to me than many others I've known. She has listened and phoned me and even remembered my birthday with a little gift. This friendship has formed only in the past two years.

"There must be other people out there who have faced or are facing the same situation and finding no support within the church. All I can say is you can make it through, but only by placing your trust in Jesus, no-one else."

So while this couple goes through the trauma of separation, the question remains: How would you and your church rate under these circumstances? What would you do that would help them? She, at least, is determined to try to get some positives out of a difficult situation.

"Both my husband and I do not want this separation to be *bitter*; we want to come out of it as two *better* people."

But, really, this is not about one woman and one man who will probably never attend your church. It's about Adventists living in Australia and New Zealand where the divorce rate is some 40 per cent. Separation and divorce will impact on your church, and probably has.

Statistically, this woman speaks of just another marriage breakdown. Personally she speaks of a tragedy and a need. She and her husband need to be treated with dignity, respect and compassion, especially by their church.

But I fear her story is not an isolated case. Why? Notice another statistic: 50 per cent of Adventists in Australia who divorce no longer attend Adventist churches after three years.

"Please don't think that I'm bitter or angry toward the church, because I'm not; my feelings are more of disappointment and sadness. Maybe this letter will give others something to discuss over lunch today."

Yes, maybe. Or maybe we could take the challenge this story illustrates and plan to make our churches caring places for hurting people, no matter what the hurt.

SEEN, BUT NOT
. . . WHAT?

Three different scenes in three different churches one Sabbath morning. Maybe you'll recognise one of them.

SCENE 1: A five-year-old walks shyly to the front of the church and stands on the spot marked out for her. She begins to recite a poem about sharing.

Two lines into the poem her voice drops, slows and then she stops. She looks down at Mum in the front pew. Mum whispers the next few words.

Memory back, confidence too, the girl moves into the rest of the poem. Her skirt swirls to the left and then to the right and then back and forth as she moves with the rhythm of her voice.

When she finishes she half-walks, half-runs back to her mother, and together they go back to their seat.

SCENE 2: It's offering time. Today the offering is being taken up by the primary school–aged sons and daughters of deacons and deaconesses. Their mothers and fathers stand beside them as they pass out the offering bags. Some look nervous. Some take this very seriously. A couple have cheeky grins.

After they finish taking up the offering they file, father–son, mother–daughter, father–daughter, mother–son, to the front of the church. They bow their heads as an elder prays over the offering.

There are no smiles now. This *is* serious.

Then the children place the offering on the table at the front of the church and go back to sit with their parents.

SCENE 3: The children's story time brings children hurrying to the front. The pastor has the story today and he's a good storyteller. You can see that the children like this part of church.

He's dramatising the story of the lost sheep, involving the children in the search for the little sheep lost in the wilderness. There are a few amused smiles from the congregation as the pastor leads the children from place to place across the front of the church in search of the sheep. They stop occasionally to listen for his cries.

Finally they discover the lost sheep. He wasn't in the wilderness after all; he was behind the organ.

Then, for a moment, the pastor quietly talks to them about how God cares for them. He asks them to put their hands up if they want to be God's person.

All hands go up.

The story over, the organist plays the introduction to a hymn as the children go back to their seats.

* * *

Maybe one of those scenes, or a variation on one of them, was played out in your church today. Why?

Nobody can remember the poem the girl recited—except her parents, who lived through the never-ending practising. All the others remember is that she scored 10 on the cuteness scale. Was it worth it?

Should the deacons be relinquishing their role into the hands of the unordained?

And are we just entertaining children (bribing them?) by having a story? In my day (at this point you're meant to feel sorry for the strict upbringing I had) all I was allowed for entertainment in church was a hymnbook and a hanky. Should it be any different now? Besides, don't those children have Sabbath school to do some of those creative, fun things?

Let's get serious about church, right?

Right! Serious enough to say to children that they are a part of the church. That it is their church as well as the grown-ups. That they will be encouraged to lisp their way through a Scripture reading, or an appropriate poem, or a simple song for the church. That they can assist the adults in the tasks of the church. That there will be a message specially designed for them.

What kind of signal does this give the children? It says that the church where this happens for them is *their* church. The church is building memories for them. The church is training them.

And just as the pastor challenges adult hearts and minds, we'll want him, and others, to ask the children for commitment as well—a commitment aimed at their level.

Asking *Why do we do this?* is always a valuable question. It's a question that should be asked about the kind of involvement that's suitable and effective for children.

In writing about "public worship," Ellen White comments: "While we worship God, we are not to consider this a drudgery. The Sabbath of the Lord is to be made a blessing to us and to our children" (*Child Guidance*, page 531).

Should children be involved in the worship service? I think I know what the One who once said, "Forbid them not," would say.

MARRIED
AND HAPPY?

I'm married to a woman who tells me she thinks I can do anything. (And why should I try to tell her anything else?) She says I'm her hero. She even considers me handsome. (Check the photo on the back cover—if you hold it up to the light and squint a lot you might see just a touch of handsome.)

Some, especially those who know me, think she's deluded, blind and/or stupid. If she is (and I haven't noticed it), I've learned to live with her disabilities—quite happily, thank you.

Our marriage came to mind a few years ago when I came to the awesome realisation that I had passed one of life's milestones: I had been married for more than half my lifetime.

If this had been written before I was married, it would probably have been called "Seven steps to the perfect marriage." But the first year of marriage knocked that out of me—neither of us know how we survived that year.

But we did survive and we learned the truth of Doug Larson's comment: "More marriages might survive if the partners realised that sometimes the better comes after the worse" (quoted in Pat Quigley and Marilyn Shroyer, *Making It Through the Night: How Couples Can Survive a Crisis Together*, Conari Press). That's certainly how it was for us.

Most of what I read, hear and see on the topic tells me that marriage is in trouble, to the point that some 40 per cent of Australian marriages end in divorce.

And the Adventist Church is obviously not free of marriage failure. I only have to look at our wedding photos to be reminded of that. Of the five others in the wedding party, four are Adventists, and two have divorced.

No-blame divorces appear to have made divorce an easy option in Australia and New Zealand. But it really isn't an *easy* option because divorce is never without emotional consequences. The marriage has failed and the husband and wife wear that failure in some form. There's an emotional cost even in the most civil of divorces. And the equation becomes even more complicated if there's dispute over the children.

It is true that, in some cases, separation is the best option—there are times when keeping the marriage going at *any* cost can be destructive or even dangerous. But separation or termination shouldn't be the first option.

Some things are worth working on. So even if you think you've married the wrong person, it may be better to try to make your marriage work rather than to try another spouse. More second marriages fail than first marriages. Fortunately, in most cases, if two people determine to make a relationship work, they can make it work

I pity those well-advertised personalities who get onto the marriage-go-round. They'll never find the true intimacy they're looking for. That kind of intimacy only comes from a relationship that's forged over years.

It's the kind of intimacy that has shared the joys, the sorrows, the contentment, the heartaches, the successes, and the failures over time. It's based on a commitment to each other that remains firm, come what may.

It's the kind of intimacy that is best found when a couple are committed to each other and to a relationship with Jesus Christ.

In this me-first world, it isn't always easy to be other-centred. But that's what commitment is about.

Here's an encouraging thought: "Study to advance the happiness of each other. Let there be mutual love, mutual forbearance. Then marriage, instead of being the end of love, will be as if it were the very beginning of love. The warmth of true friendship, the love that binds heart to heart, is a foretaste of the joys of heaven" (*Happiness Homemade*, page 24).

It's time for those of us who are joyously married to come out of the closet and admit it—and show it. Having flesh-and-blood examples of the fact that marriage can be fun, stimulating, satisfying, exciting and joyous may be the only way to counter the statistics and the bad press marriage receives.

Others may then pause and say, "If it can work for them, it can work for me."

PERMANENT
OUTCASTS?

"Eleven years ago an Adventist church decided that it could get along without me," says a letter I received in a letter to the editor. "For the past six years I have tried, without success, to rejoin the church in four different locations. My application has only reached the church board once; church members have never been given the opportunity to vote."

The writer never reveals why the church "decided that it could get along without me." But that isn't the point. Do we make it too hard for former members to become members again? Is this person's experience being repeated elsewhere?

"As a church, we preach love, forgiveness and acceptance," continues the writer, "and quite rightly so, for it is the standard of God's Word. Yet in practice, the church, its ministers and some church board members, are locked into a policy that doesn't allow them to forgive and accept ex-members back into the church.

"This policy does not allow acceptance back into the church without the consent of the church that disfellowshipped the person, and that opens the gate to all sorts of abuses. Combine this with change of ministers, ministers and members that are unforgiving and you have an ex-member who stays that way."

Wait a minute, there's no policy that says that consent is needed from the church that took disciplinary action against a member before he or she can become a member in another church (check the *Seventh-day Adventist Church Manual*). The manual does suggest that people should be readmitted, if possible, in the church that dismissed them.

Much more serious than these technicalities are the accusations about adopting an attitude that doesn't allow us to forgive and thus prevents us from accepting ex-members back into the church. Surely we would do better to assume that time and maturity have made a difference rather than allow long memories to dictate our response.

Do we apply a double standard and discriminate between former and prospective members? Are we harsher on former members than prospective members?

"In one of the churches I attended where I applied for membership," says the writer, "I taught a Sabbath school class and combined Sabbath school classes. I was asked to wait awhile. I waited over three years, during which time the pastor changed three times, but the result was still the same,

"The same happened in another church where I applied for membership. After attending for nine months, teaching Sabbath school classes for three months, and taking combined lessons, and being invited to participate in the worship service, and listening to a lot of sermons on love, forgiveness and acceptance, I withdrew my application for membership."

Surely we have a responsibility when members have been disfellowshipped, that the church should, where possible, keep in touch with them and manifest a spirit of friendship and love, endeavouring to win them back to the fold.

And that thought isn't original with me; it's virtually word for word from the *SDA Church Manual* from the chapter entitled "Church discipline"—it's worth reading.

I reread this letter several times and every time I sensed something of the frustration the writer obviously feels. The writer wants to rejoin the Adventist Church.

Read this: "I am talking about any avenue to re-enter the church: baptism, profession of faith, or standing on my head and singing 'Jesus loves me,' whatever. I have changed churches *and* states, all to no avail."

There may well be a valid reason why the letter writer can't rejoin the Seventh-day Adventist Church; I don't know. But if there is, common decency (and a dozen biblical injunctions) dictates that the person needs to know what it is and not be left clinging to some vain hope.

It would be easy to dismiss this letter by saying that we're hearing only one side of the story. And we are, but there's value in reflecting on whether we too harbour some fault.

Do we represent Christ well in these circumstances? It would be a terrible thing to fall under the condemnation of Matthew 6:15.

FAIR GO,
PEW SITTER

We pew sitters can be pretty tough on our preachers. (Yes, I do get the opportunity to sit in the pew and listen to the preachers.) But then, our preachers rarely preach the right kind of sermon. Right? When was the last time you heard a sermon that really fitted your needs? That made you weep, made you laugh, made you think? That affirmed the fundamental beliefs? That uplifted Christ in such a way that we could envision Him on the cross? That showed a social conscience? That touched the children and the aged? That left you wanting the preacher to continue when the sermon had finished?

Can you remember *any* sermon that had all those elements? No wonder the preacher is served for Sabbath lunch. When will he ever get it right? (I'm using *he* because most preachers are male.)

Or are we unfair in expecting this each Sabbath? Do we act like some cricket commentator who sits in a box overlooking the field and tells us exactly how each ball should have been bowled, or better played? There's a reason why the commentators are in the box and not on the field.

It's time to give the preachers a fair go.

Church isn't TV

Pity the preacher. All week many of us have watched fast-paced programs on the television. And most programs have mega-dollars available for production.

The poor preacher stands before us almost naked by comparison. He may have a felt pen and whiteboard, but little else. We live in a visually oriented society—no matter what he uses as a visual aid, he can't compete with what we're used to.

Television makes us brain-lazy. Its message attacks the senses in many ways. To get the message from the preacher requires concentration. That's hard for some of us. So let's not criticise the preacher just because he isn't as dramatic as our favourite TV program.

Do we listen?

Not only do we listen, but do we listen as if the preacher is the Lord's anointed? Let's never assume that the preacher for the day is there simply to fill the air with words. If the Lord is with the preacher, and we must believe that He is, the words the preacher speaks may well be the most important we hear all week. We must listen.

Are we looking?

Are we looking for a word from the Lord? Do we get so hung up about how a thing is said, or that something was said that *sounded* suspect, that we missed what God had to say to us?

Or are we preoccupied with the preacher's unusual mannerisms, his wife, crumpled suit and the way that he felt uncomfortable telling a children's story? Is that what we were looking for when we came to church? Let's look for a word from the Lord.

Are we prepared?

"Those who assemble to worship Him should put away every evil thing. Unless they worship Him in spirit and truth and in the beauty of holiness, their coming together will be of no avail" (*Prophets and Kings*, page 50). That kind of preparation has nothing to do with the preacher.

Could it be that if we aren't hearing the preacher, it's because of what we've got running in our own lives. Let's plan to come to worship, prepared with a clean heart and prepared to focus our eyes on the Master, not the servant.

Do we participate?

Worship is a joint activity, something shared between the preacher and the congregation. If we, the pew sitters, worship as mere spectators, we'll rarely find that the sermon speaks to us.

Being like a cricket commentator isn't the role of the pew sitter. The commentator is detached from the game. The commentator makes comparisons, gives statistics and describes the event, but still isn't a part of the game. When we sit in the pew, we're on the playing field. We're a part of the team in which the preacher for the day is the captain.

The point is, we're on the same team as the preacher. When we realise that, we pew sitters may find that our focus is more on winning the game than chewing on the captain.

FAIR GO, PREACHER

We preachers carry an awesome responsibility. When we preach, we stand before the people as God's representative.

Our responsibility is twofold: to be true to the calling to preach that we've been given, and to effectively communicate God's Word to the people. I have asked pew sitters to give their preachers a fair go. But we preachers need to give the pew sitters a fair go as well.

Preach the Word

Those of us who have been ordained know that part of our ordination commitment is to preach the Word. Anything less and we belittle the worship hour. Let's search for ways to best illustrate and best explain the Word—illustrations from world news, the latest psychological and sociological findings and historical research are all valid. But we go too far if these illustrations become the centre of the preaching.

Neither is the preaching time meant for pet theories, pet theology or pet prophecies. It's meant for the preaching of the Word and for uplifting the focus of that Word, Jesus Christ.

Take the time

Most preachers are busy people. But if preparing the sermon has taken a low priority, listening to it will take a lower priority.

An hour's preparation on Friday night (or, worse, Sabbath morning) just isn't good enough. Why should preachers be taken seriously if they aren't serious about preparing for preaching?

There is only one hour each week when the congregation is together—Sabbath morning worship time. This time is important. We cheat our congregations if we haven't taken the *time* to be properly prepared.

Enthusiasm

It's hard for the congregation to get excited about something that the preacher isn't enthusiastic about. Conversational-style preaching may be in, but we don't have to yell, thump the desk or stalk across the pulpit area to show enthusiasm. The listeners will pick up the enthusiasm if the preacher is enthusiastic.

With the best news ever (the good news) as the basis for our preaching, shouldn't we be a little bit excited?

Powerful preaching

Powerful preaching only comes when we preachers are plugged into the power source. And this means that we need to organise our lives so that we spend time with God.

From that base we can better follow the command that includes preaching: "Whatever your hand finds to do, do it with all your might . . ." (Ecclesiastes 9:10).

Live the life

The worst advertisement of all, for our preaching, is if we say one thing in the pulpit and live something else outside. The old proverb "What you do speaks so loud that I can't hear what you say" is especially true for preachers.

Let's never set ourselves up as if we believe that we're the perfect example of Christian living. We're with the pew sitters in this life pilgrimage. We preachers are still learning too.

And we should live a life consistent with the Christian qualities we espouse.

Keep it relevant

The best preachers for congregations should be local pastors, because they should know the people best. The best preaching is practical and relevant to the needs of the congregation.

Whenever and wherever we preach, we should ask ourselves, "Is what I'm preaching going to make a difference to anyone? Is it going to help the listeners face a sometimes-ugly world? Will my words make Christ more real to the listeners?"

Variety

Variety in preaching content and style is particularly important for those who regularly preach in one church. Just as a one note piano would soon be tiresome, so it is with a one-theme preacher. Variety in preaching is a recognition of the various needs of the congregation.

Writing this probably means I've focused on my own weaknesses, and I'm not sure if I dare preach again. But we preachers (even part-time ones) love a challenge—that's why we preach.

THE WORLD
HAS CHANGED

THE WORLD
HAS CHANGED

The world has changed. Terrorism has written its message in fire, blood and rubble. CNN and the others delivered it to our homes—again and again.

The world has changed. It's far more serious than what's happened to the skyline of New York. More sinister than the lives of families directly impacted by the tragedy, or the impact on the United States.

Terrorism demonstrated the will and the sophistication to pull off complex acts of destruction to make an entire nation—any nation—feel unsafe. Terrorism recognises no borders. It is deadly serious and seriously deadly.

We're used to tit-for-tat terrorist acts in the Middle East, the occasional attack in Europe or those by the IRA. But they pale compared to what we've witnessed in New York and Washington. And the impact has been magnified through the millions worldwide who watched it "live" on television. Add to that the billions who watched the replays.

Is there any safe place on the planet?

I close my eyes and I still see the Boeing 767 slicing into the south tower of the World Trade Center, exploding in a ball of flame. That image, and others, will stay. Terrorism has made its statement.

The world has changed.

Apocalyptic overtones?

Is this the first step toward Armageddon? Probably not, but time will answer that question. We must be cautious about claiming too much, for these terrorists are extremists who have relatively few open supporters. The present danger of some kind of holocaust is more likely to come from the reaction of the United States and its allies. Besides, even if it proves to be part of a *jihad* (holy war), this act appears to be more political than religious. The message from apocalyptic passages of the Bible is that the final conflict is over spiritual and religious issues. In simple terms, it comes down to God and His people against a Satan-dominated world—that's the great controversy's final chapter.

Caution is also needed in any attempt to link this act of terrorism with Ellen White's comments about burning skyscrapers in New York, something seen many times in the past century. Let's take her statement no further than she intended (see *Testimonies for the Church*, Vol 9, pages 12, 13).

Certainly, this terrorist attack is another sign of the times (reread Matthew 24), a reminder that Jesus' return is not far away. It's a reminder—if we needed one—that evil and sin are in full evidence on this planet. It's a reminder that we live on a planet in need of a Saviour. And at the personal level, it's a reminder of how fragile life is. We do need to keep that relationship with Christ, for only in Him is life eternal.

Where was God?

If God is all-powerful, why . . . ? A baby with cerebral palsy. Children starving in Africa. A terrorist attack leaving thousands dead. The question fits them all—and more.

Could He have stopped the attack? Yes. Why didn't He? We don't know.

We *do* know it wasn't the fault, or sin, of those killed. Jesus turns us from that conclusion in His comments about Galileans killed by Pilate and those killed by a falling tower (Luke 13:1-5). We *do* know God grieves these deaths. We *do* know His original plan had no place for death, and neither does His eternal plan; death is an aberration. We *do* know God has demonstrated His love, even for terrorists, in the most dramatic way possible.

But while such thoughts may satisfy our intellect, when we turn on the television and see another body bag carried from the rubble, we wonder. Then there's the small voice that says, "Trust Me." So we hold on to Him, in faith, and dare to let God be God, allowing Him to deal with the horrors of evil—in His time.

What can we do?

Pray. Pray for those who have lost family and friends.

Pray for cool heads and wisdom from US leaders, and their allies, as they plan to react to what they have declared is war.

Pray for those who believe they have to kill to make a point.

Pray for understanding in our own communities lest there be outbreaks of racial violence.

Pray that this experience will increase our own desire to live for and serve the God of heaven, the ultimate Peacemaker.

Pray for peace.

Pray, Thy kingdom come! That's when the world will change again, this time according to God's plan.

ELVIS, DOLLY
AND A DILEMMA

Elvis may have left the building, but some are planning his encore. In fact, a petition is being circulated demanding his return. An Internet web site—Americans for Cloning Elvis (ACE)—is a product of Elvis Presley fan Bob Meyer, on which he urges all red-white-and-blue Americans to insist their government clone him (Elvis, that is).

Dolly the sheep, born after cloning in 1997, has opened a new chapter in scientific history. A scary chapter. It may have taken 276 tries to clone the Scottish ewe, but that figure will improve with practice. Will it now go from sheep to shepherd? From ewe to you? (Just two of the titles of articles printed in *The Bulletin* and *Time*. At the time both magazines ran five articles on the topic—recognition of the importance of this breakthrough.)

The cloning of animals and humans is not a new thought. This was the basis of the Hollywood blockbuster *Jurassic Park*. The 1970s film *The Boys from Brazil* featured the cloning of Adolf Hitler. Are we about to enter Aldous Huxley's "brave new world" (his book of this title was published more than 70 years ago)?

Is it really possible for humans to be cloned?

Yes, possible—and soon, says Ian Wilmut of the Roslin Institute in Edinburgh, Scotland. Wilmut headed the team that cloned Dolly.

"I think now to contemplate using our present technique with humans would be inhuman," he told the media. "It need not happen, and I hope it will not."

The Church of Scotland was quick to condemn such thinking, as was the Vatican and Bill Clinton. Lois Pines, a US state senator, told the *Boston Business Journal*: "They call the first cloned animal Dolly, but she might just as well have been named Pandora."

The moral problems of cloning a human forced a Belgian hospital to quickly deny it had "accidentally" cloned a child. This was "a fantasy triggered by Dolly," Professor Robert Schoysman told the Reuters news agency.

The English government, which bankrolled the research, is so nervous it has already halved Wilmut's present funding and will withdraw it completely next year. But Wilmut's team has had offers from several businesses to keep going. He's promised to introduce us to a cloned cow before the end of the year.

Will we get Elvis or Einstein or Florence Nightingale back? Carl Felbaun, the president of the US Biotechnology Industry Organisation, told CNN, "I would assert this is not a line we want to cross. I would say this is not even a line we want to approach."

But there is still a dilemma. If it can be done, it probably will be done. Science is not good at asking the "should we?" question. It tends to focus on the "can we?" Which means that, probably, the line will be crossed sometime soon. Not with Elvis, however, for, currently, live tissue is needed (Elvis is dead, isn't he?).

There are various arguments for cloning humans: Childless couples (even gay couples) could have a child; there's a chance for medical research and the harvesting of body parts; or a couple could replace a child who has died.

Wilmut helps bring us back to reality. He told the English parliament, "The idea that you can bring back a child, that you can bring back a father—it is nonsensical. You can make a genetically identical copy, but you can't get the person back."

As far as medical research and body parts are concerned, a cloned human will be human. Do we maim or kill one human to help another? Another ethical problem.

There will be some who see cloning as their best chance at immortality. While the new person may not be them, genetically they will live on. For some that will be enough and, if it only takes money, it's a cheap price to pay.

Human cloning would be one of those giant steps for science, but it shouldn't impact on our faith. In cloning there is no creation of life from nothing (*ex nihilo*). The genetic structure was already in place in the cells used to create Dolly. She had to go through the normal processes of gestation and birth and growth.

The cloning of plants has been an accepted practice for some time. Dolly was a next logical step. Will humans be cloned? Probably.

And when it happens it will be so important to grasp the two truths found in John: "Through him [Jesus] all things were made; without him nothing was made that has been made. In him was life, and that life was the light of men" (John 1:3, 4).

Jesus is the out-of-nothing Creator and spiritual re-creator. Science is no match for either.

QUESTIONS FROM
A KILLING FIELD

Port Arthur, a popular tourist destination in Tasmania, became a killing field on April 28, 1996. Gunman Martin Bryant murdered 35 people in a brief but deadly shooting spree. For days news reporters talked specifically about a "numbness" in Tasmania and other parts of Australia as people tried to come to terms with the horrific event.

Then there was anger. The anger was aimed, naturally, at the perpetrator.

And then there was a search for blame. Was the killer of a sound mind? Early on there were suggestions in the press that he had had psychological problems. How then was he allowed to purchase firearms?

The depth of reaction to the event was highlighted by the unusual swiftness with which the federal and state governments acted on gun laws. Semiautomatic guns were banned in Australia, and this before the gun lobby could raise a significant protest.

For those of us not personally touched by the tragedy, we seemed to be coming to terms with it—and then another reminder confronted us. I remember the funeral of the mother and her two little daughters. The sadness came into our living rooms; in the face of the husband and father.

We were confronted again as the massacre in all its gruesome details were raked over during the trial. A trial that took weeks.

Some suggested it would have been more merciful if the killer had turned the gun on himself and become the 36th victim.

Two questions

Where was God? The question usually sounds like this: "If God really is all powerful, why didn't He *do* something?"

Unless we have a proper understanding of God and the forces of evil, we will tend to take a position that says that there is no God, or that God is schizophrenic—both good and bad.

The Bible begins with God, and in the third chapter we are introduced to an enemy. The emphasis Adventists have placed on the great controversy theme (the battle between good and evil, God and Satan) is important in helping us understand how an event such as the Port Arthur massacre was possible.

God took a risk when He created our planet and peopled it. He allowed freedom of choice. And that freedom extended to the point where we could reject Him and His ways. This freedom shouldn't surprise us if He is a God of love, for that's what love allows.

It explains why such a horrific event as that described in Revelation 12 took place. War in heaven! This freedom of choice extends to the very throne room of God. And it was abused.

There are times when God acts to override evil. You'll find God's intervening acts in the Bible and in history. Mostly, though, God has allowed the "sin experiment" to work its own way through. God allows most choices, for good or evil, to have their natural consequence.

This doesn't explain why God did not choose to act in this case. But it does shift the blame.

Looking beyond Port Arthur, we do see Him at work restoring people to His kingdom. For the love He has is big enough to give us another chance in another choice: "[God] . . . gave his one and only Son . . . not . . . to condemn the world, but to save the world through him" (John 3:16, 17).

The Port Arthur massacre should make us long for Him to return and establish His kingdom of peace.

The other question is one I didn't hear expressed. Can we forgive him—the killer?

Do not misunderstand me. I'm not belittling the crime. Our sympathies should be firmly with the victims' families and loved ones. We need to grieve with them, to support and encourage them. If nothing more, they need our prayer support. In a brief rampage they were dealt a lifetime blow.

But can we forgive? Once we saw his face in the newspapers and on television, we had a better target for our rage. Yet if we maintain and nurture hatred, we harm only ourselves.

It's better to see him as a person who needs help. We need to remind ourselves that whoever the perpetrator of whatever crime, basic Christianity demands forgiveness. There comes a time when we need to look beyond the horror of the deed and see the confused person behind the deed.

The two questions: The first is about whether we're still willing to trust God. The second challenges our commitment to the ways of Jesus.

BEING CHRISTIAN
ABOUT SUICIDE

Over the past couple of years I've sat with three families who have lost a loved one through suicide. In each case those who died were in the prime of life and, it seemed, had much to live for.

I've sensed the awful blackness that comes upon family members and friends as they try to cope. Death is tragic enough. Self-inflicted death is so much harder to understand, so much harder to move beyond.

The fact that, in these cases, those who suicided were not active Adventists makes no difference to the tragedy involved.

You probably don't need to be reminded that suicide is on the increase in Australia and New Zealand. Current statistics say that Australia has the highest rate of youth suicides in the Western world. It may reach into a friend's family or, God forbid, into your family. I've learned some things about suicide in these past few years:

If only . . .

The guilt felt by those left behind is incredible. It's often expressed by "If only . . ." If only they'd been there. If only they'd known what was in his/her mind. If only they'd realised how serious the situation was. They see the waste of years of active life they may have been able to have preserved.

Sure, if someone had been there things might have been different.

Then again it may simply have delayed the event. Nobody knows.

Understanding the concept of being our "brother's keeper" may make what I'm about to say sound harsh, but I want to say it as emphatically as I can: *We can't be responsible for another person's decision or actions.* As tragic as suicide may be, it is that person's decision. And the responsibility for that act must remain with the one who made the decision.

Our churches must be open and available for families and friends to say goodbye to a loved one who has suicided. Our hearts must be open to the hurts they feel. Our support must be available, particularly through the first year after the death.

Let God decide

The children understood that their father had taken his life—the oldest must have been about 10 years old. They wanted me to take the funeral as a way of asking God to look after Dad.

I don't expect you to appreciate the theology behind what they were asking, and it wasn't the time to give a study on salvation and the state of the dead. But the concept is 100 per cent correct—we need to leave decisions of salvation in God's hands.

It's too easy for us to condemn one who has suicided. But who made us judge? That's God's prerogative. God's ways are not our ways. His wisdom is far greater, His understanding much deeper.

And don't dismiss this as some kind of feel-good theology. This is reality theology—biblical theology. We humans have only a limited view. We see the externals; God sees the heart. He knows the trauma within.

Christ purposely reached out to those with dark corners in their life; He understood them. That hasn't changed.

Let's leave God to be the judge of whether someone who suicided is part of His kingdom. Matthew 7:1 should be enough warning.

Support needed

Talking to these families has been among the more sobering times I've experienced. Any death confronts us with our own mortality. Suicide confronts us with so much more. Questions come: Is *my* life worth living? What philosophy of life have I developed that makes it worth living? Where does God fit?

Facing these questions can help us grow in maturity. And, often, the family and friends of the one who suicided want to talk about those kind of issues.

It's important that we demonstrate Christlike qualities of understanding and compassion as we help others through this difficult situation. So often they are confused, embarrassed and don't know where to turn. We must be willing to be there. Willing to listen, even if they choose to tell what happened. You may not want to hear, and you certainly don't need the images in your head. But this may be the best support through this crisis.

And that's something else I learned from these experiences. As members of the body of Christ rallied to support these people in positive ways, the gifts, skills and abilities available helped dramatically through the early, difficult times and encouraged long-term healing.

Surely that's what being church is about (see Matthew 25:34-46).

LESSONS FROM WACO—1

The following appears here as it did in the May 22, 1993, Record *to maintain the sense of immediacy that it had coming just after the Waco tragedy.*

The Adventist Church has rightly distanced itself from the Branch Davidian of Seventh-day Adventist sect involved in the siege in Waco, Texas. But one of the tragedies is that the Branch Davidians recruited followers from the Adventist Church. Some followers from this division were caught in the siege.

We investigated the impact of the Branch Davidians on the church in an attempt to uncover how church members could be deceived into following such a blatantly unchristian sect. There is no simple answer, but there are lessons to learn:

1. Basic Christian teaching

There seems to have been a lack of basic biblical understanding by those who became involved in the Branch Davidians. We may be emphasising the distinctive Adventist doctrines, but downplaying the importance of fundamental Christian and biblical beliefs. We need to emphasise both.

2. Not all are misfits

It's incorrect, and too easy, to say that only misfits in society and the Adventist Church will be caught out by a sect like the Branch Davidians. Some may fit that category, but not all. Most are just misguided.

I emphasise this point for fear that we may be tempted to say that those who have been lost to the Branch Davidians were in some way strange. Some have made a positive contribution to the church and would still be doing so if they had not been caught up in this sect.

This point came home with force when my daughter reminded me that she and one of the girls caught in the siege became friends just before the girl's involvement with the Branch Davidians. This girl may have been brainwashed, but she was no misfit. (She died in the fire.)

3. Assurance of salvation

We have been hesitant to speak of the assurance we can have of salvation. This has been reinforced by the inappropriate use of comments made by Ellen White warning us against saying, "I am saved." Her warning is not against the assurance of present salvation, but against those who would adopt a once-saved-always-saved position. In the context of her warnings she says, "It is he that endureth unto the end that shall be saved" (*Selected Messages*, Book 1, page 315). She speaks strongly of Christian assurance.

Individuals who know they are accepted by God will be less inclined to go searching for something extra. We need to emphasise that we can have the assurance of salvation now. There are no doubts about our salvation when we are in Christ. And as long as we remain in Christ we have salvation.

4. More than charisma

Those I have talked to who have met him are unanimous—David Koresh (Vernon Howell) was charismatic. Naturally, not everyone who is charismatic is evil or has evil intent, but we need to look beyond the charisma. We need to be Berean-like in testing and checking any new teaching or teacher.

5. Back to the Bible

This may be obvious, but if we know what the Bible says we will be less likely fooled by someone who comes with false teaching.

6. The middle ground

An important lesson we need to learn from the infiltration by the Branch Davidians is to be on our guard. There are others out there who claim to have new light or old light for us. The church (and I'm talking about the local church) needs to be aware of what is happening on the local scene and assess its impact on the people and the program of the church.

This is not a call for a witch-hunt, but it is a call to develop, emphasise, uphold and defend middle-ground Adventism.

7. Our focus

The focus of our preaching, teaching, discussion and thinking needs to be on Jesus Christ. He alone is the way, the truth and the life. Without Him we won't know the way, we'll believe a lie and, in extreme cases, we'll see death.

LESSONS FROM WACO—2

The following appears here as it did in the May 29, 1993, Record to maintain the sense of immediacy that it had coming just after the Waco tragedy.

This should be a time of heart searching for the Adventist Church. While we can distance ourselves from the teachings and militancy of the Waco Branch Davidians, many caught in the siege were at one time Seventh-day Adventists.

Dare we now quietly purge our church rolls of those connected with the Branch Davidians? Dare we hope that the problem will go away? And hope that nobody has noticed? The connection has been noticed. We can't hide it. And we ignore it at our own peril.

1. A chance to be Christlike

All caught by the Branch Davidians are now in mourning. They had friends who died in the fire. Our first responsibility is to offer comfort, support and friendship to help them through this tragedy. We, the church, were once home for many of them. They may have rejected us, but we now have a real opportunity to demonstrate that we haven't rejected them—an opportunity to demonstrate that the church is bigger than any embarrassment caused by the Davidian connection.

If our motivation, though, is to win them back to the church, we may be disappointed. If our motivation is to act as Christ would, our reward will be in being true to His calling.

2. Keep prophecy biblical

The question needs to be asked: Have we encouraged extremism in understanding the biblical teaching of the remnant or the end-time prophecies? There's a valid place for teaching and understanding the prophecies. But it is *not* valid to become so speculative or extreme that we end up with a perverted view of the remnant and events surrounding the Second Coming.

Praise God, we came out of a movement based on prophecy. But let's maintain a mature, biblical understanding of prophecy. We aren't called to chase down every conspiracy theory as if it were the latest end-time sign. Christ called us to be aware of trends (like noticing that the fig tree is telling us that summer is near—Matthew 24:32, 33), not to be concerned about every hiccup on the international scene. We must not read more into the biblical text than is there.

Fortunately middle-ground Adventism has, in the main, held to a conservative, biblical and historic Protestant position in prophetic interpretations. There is safety in this.

3. Have we lost our purpose?

The Davidians may have had a perverted doctrine, but they had set goals and a set purpose. One of the attractions of a sect is their clearly defined mission.

Their mission may have been outrageous and befuddled, but it was clearly understood by the believers. And that purpose was emphasised time and again by the leaders.

While we would reject anything to do with mindless following or brainwashing, there's a place for articulating more fully what we're about.

The gospel is clear. The task we have, as Christ's followers, is clear. The reason for our being is clear. But have we successfully put this into words and actions?

"If the church became a movement again," says Martin Marty in *Christianity Today*, "and if we felt a life-and-death urgency about getting the message out and getting it right, we would probably not be discussing how long we should go on" (March 8, 1993). That kind of urgency and purpose would make it hard for any group to infiltrate our churches.

4. Building the camaraderie

Related to this sense of purpose is the sense of camaraderie built up among the followers in a sect. Many are caught in a sect through the desire to feel wanted, needed and loved—something they may feel is missing in their local church.

This is a challenge—let's not ignore it. The best thing we can do is give serious study to Acts 2:42-47 to learn how the early church achieved this sense of belonging—even when the local Jerusalem church had a membership of several thousand.

Biblical truth is important, but even truth is cold and uninviting unless the people who share it are warm and friendly. The church is important, but the church can seem aloof and distant unless the people in it are approachable and open.

Christ was people-centred throughout His ministry. Surely that gives us a clue as to what we, His people, should be.

ON SEXUAL ABUSE

At this, the beginning of National Child Protection Week in Australia, it seems appropriate to attempt something positive about a topic opened up through the News and Letters pages a few months ago—sexual abuse.

Not everyone was happy with us for allowing the topic of sexual abuse to be discussed through the pages of the *Record*. That's OK. At times we've felt uncomfortable too. If it has generated awareness and signalled to those who have been abused that it is all right to talk about it, we may have taken a major step in a healing direction.

When we bring subjects out into the open—even ones that make us feel uncomfortable—we begin to reveal them for what they are and can show the trauma they bring.

I fear two things. I fear we may be tempted to say sexual abuse is such an insignificant problem in the church that we should ignore it. "Let's get on with the *real* work of the church," I can hear someone say. Sorry, but the real work of the church is people—and their hurts.

Insignificant problem? Even if we accept the 5 per cent figure some have suggested for the number of cases of sexual abuse within the church (and that figure seems too low), that's one person for every 20 in the church in Australia and New Zealand. How many *could* that be in your church? It's almost 15 in mine.

I've another fear that some may want to set up a witch-hunt in an attempt to rid the church of this evil once and for all. Don't. That won't help.

We have reported in *Record* on seminars and published official statements about sexual abuse. For those of us who had never suffered from sexual abuse this was fairly clinical stuff. Then came a letter to the editor that challenged whether we can take figures from outside the church and assume that the same occurs within the church. And, to be fair to the writer, it was probably a question that many of us asked.

Suddenly, for me, this was no longer a clinical issue. Several women who had suffered sexual abuse wrote to me. Two even phoned me. They all had a common, emphatic message: "It's real. It's in the church. And if you're looking for statistics, I'm one."

For these women the abuse had finished several years before, but they're still trying to come to terms with what happened.

Women and men who have been sexually abused, and children or teens being sexually abused are good at covering the pain. They've usually had experience at hiding the facts from others.

I was stunned to receive a phone call from someone I knew and hear her, through her tears, tell me of the abuse she had suffered. No-one would have known. In fact, no-one believed her when she tried to tell others.

It may be hard to listen, but that's what we need to do. Not accepting the reality of what they have experienced only abuses them again. We need to be aware that our own feelings may make it hard to hear what they are saying.

Sexual abuse is a double-sided issue. The perpetrator of sexual abuse needs help. These people have a serious problem if they think this is an acceptable way of achieving intimacy. And if they don't think it's acceptable, they're carrying guilt that may destroy them.

To both the one who has been, or is being, abused and the perpetrator I say: Please seek professional help.

One of the more positive things has been the number of people offering assistance or a listening ear to those who have suffered from abuse. Those offers of assistance are currently being assessed by people with expertise in sexual-abuse counselling.

We shouldn't be surprised if we find some of the problems of society within the church. We demonstrate that we are followers of Jesus not by denying that we have problems, but in how we handle those problems.

GUN CONTROL—
VAIN HOPE?

Twelve-year-old Casey Sidebottom marched Melbourne streets in June 1996 to protest against gun control. His picture appeared in the *Sunday Herald Sun* the day after the event, causing quite a stir because he wore his Scout uniform. Scouts are forbidden to take a political stance.

"There are 32,000 Scouts in uniform in Victoria," said Dion Ellis, Victoria's executive director of Scouts Australia; "31,999 did not turn up to a pro-gun rally. I think we should remember that."

There were *60,000* marching with him (the Vietnam War brought out 70,000 in Melbourne) and significant numbers marching in other cities. There is strong opposition to proposed Australian laws banning semiautomatic and pump-action guns (automatic weapons are already banned). Only 15,000 turned up in support of the new laws. Surveys, however, show overwhelming community support for the legislation.

Before you read further, you need to know I loathe guns. I grew up in the country where guns were common—a farmer's tool. I've used guns and I've never had a bad experience with them, but I've always felt uneasy with them. I think that's because a gun is designed specifically to kill. Killing for sport is something I find abhorrent. (I appreciate the skill involved in target shooting.)

Having declared myself, let me now add that the pro-gun lobby makes some valid points. They claim they've become victims of the Port Arthur massacre in Tasmania, the trigger for new laws. They're right. Even the Prime Minister has apologised to them—the law-abiding gun owner is not to blame for this or any other murder.

A gun is only an instrument; it's the person who is the killer. It is true, however, that if the Port Arthur killer's weapon had been a screwdriver or a knife or even a bolt-action rifle, the wholesale slaughter could not have taken place.

"I disagree," says David Tipple, the Adventist owner of Gun City (and a church elder) in New Zealand. "A bolt-action rifle [which will not be banned] can fire three shots in five seconds. Guns aren't the issue. Remember, when you outlaw guns, only outlaws have guns."

He wonders if legislation will do anything—suggesting that less than half of all guns in the community were currently registered anyway. This legislation will impact specifically on those who have "done the right thing" by registering their guns and, he believes, will only send more firearms underground.

"And you have to remember, criminals don't buy guns," he adds; "they steal them or make them."

Mass murderers, he points out, have used other tools that no-one has tried to ban: matches, explosives and poison, for instance.

Fortunately, the civil liberties argument doesn't seem to be taken seriously. It is a nonsense argument. The structures of society are not at risk if certain types of guns are banned, any more than they are because marijuana is banned or 10-year-olds are refused a driver's licence.

But, to be honest, the gun bans aren't going to solve too much. The basic problem is with the person who will perform such an awful act as that seen at Port Arthur.

Our society can't stand blameless. There are issues and tremendous pressures that do lead some to extreme action. And there are individuals within society with a propensity to violence who shouldn't have access to weapons of any kind. The law may at least keep semiautomatic weapons out of their hands.

Calls to investigate movie violence is a recognition that society seems to encourage violent behaviour. The fact that violence has become entertainment must have some impact. Several studies say there is no link between screen and real violence, yet many "copycat killings" are linked to certain films.

Casey Sidebottom won't be allowed to legally own a semiautomatic rifle. During the march he carried a banner asking, "What did *I* do?" The answer is, nothing.

But the Port Arthur massacre can't be ignored; we have to try to do something. Restricting guns is *trying* to do something. That's why it has my support. That's why I will happily pay the extra tax levy to buy back those guns.

David Tipple and I may disagree about gun laws, but we do agree that a real difference will be made only with a change in values and morality in society. David says that's the real challenge facing anyone who claims Christ as Lord.

Jesus called us to be light and salt in a sometimes dark and tasteless world. Can we make a greater difference than gun laws will?